The Computer Support Directory

Voice, Fax, and Online Access Numbers

Bill Adler, Jr.
Kristy Fraser

McGraw-Hill, Inc.

New York   San Francisco   Washington, D.C.   Auckland   Bogotá   Caracas
Lisbon   London   Madrid   Mexico City   Milan   Montreal   New Delhi
San Juan   Singapore   Sydney   Tokyo   Toronto

©1995 by **Adler & Robin Books, Inc.**
Published by McGraw-Hill, Inc.

pbk   1 2 3 4 5 6 7 8 9 0 DOC/DOC 9 9 8 7 6 5

Library of Congress Cataloging-in-Publication Data
Adler, Bill, Jr.
    The computer support directory : voice, fax, and online access
    numbers / by Bill Adler, Jr. and Kristy Fraser.
        p. cm.
    Includes index.
    ISBN 0-07-000482-X
    1. Computers—Directories.   2. Computer software-
-Directories.   3. Customer service—Directories.   I. Fraser, Kristy.
II. Title.
QA76.215.A34 1995
004'.023—dc20   94-47306
                                                                        CIP

Acquisitions editor: Brad E. Schepp
Editorial team: Robert E. Ostrander, Executive Editor
                        John Baker, Book Editor
Production team: Katherine G. Brown, Director
                        Wanda S. Ditch, Desktop Operator
                        Jodi L. Tyler, Indexer
Designer: Jaclyn J. Boone   AD01

Contents

Acknowledgments

We would like to thank all of the computer-guru technicians and support representatives who provided us with concise, prompt information regarding their computer support programs. We also thank the support technicians who provided us with interviews. Exceptionally helpful and who later became prominent sources for extensive research were Bill Kalegeros of Axik Computers and Jim Ferrel of Sierra On-Line. Additional thanks also goes to Ferrel for his contribution of the troubleshooting guide.

Finally, we would like to thank all of the people from McGraw-Hill, Inc. who were involved with this book: Brad Schepp, Stacey Spurlock, Bob Ostrander, John Baker, Katherine Brown, and everyone in the McGraw-Hill, Inc. Production Department.

Introduction

The first rule of computers is never to install new software, or plug in a new computer late on a Friday afternoon. When something goes wrong, there won't be anybody around to help you.

That's what you might have thought. In reality, there are dozens of people standing by the telephone to give you just the answers that you're looking for. Some of these computer support lines are available through toll-free numbers, some you have to pay for, and others are available by calling a 900 number. Some of these services are provided only to registered users; others are open to the public at large. Still other technical support people can be reached by 24-hour fax, through online services such as CompuServe, Prodigy, the Internet and America OnLine, and on vendor bulletin boards.

If you've ever called a technical support line with a daunting dilemma, you might have discovered that the person at the other end of the phone doesn't have the answer (though he thinks he does.) That happens frequently with Windows programs (they're all interconnected in complicated, almost mystifying ways). After several calls, you finally find the right person with the correct solution. Wouldn't it be nice to have several technical support numbers from different companies that you could call?

Now, for the first time, there's one place to look to find out where to get the help you need. *The Computer Support Directory* has the telephone, fax, and TTD numbers of nearly every IBM/DOS hardware and software company in the country. *The Computer Support Directory* also includes the computer bulletin board and online service numbers and addresses for these companies.

Many computer companies have 24-hour service (something they don't advertise in their manual); many have 24-hour fax information lines. Numerous computer companies also have overseas numbers. You'll find all of this information in *The Computer Support Directory*. From now on, you'll never be alone with your computer staring you in the face, saying merely GENERAL PROTECTION FAULT. ABORT RETRY FAIL? There's help out there. Now you know where to find it.

3Com Corp.

- ▶ 3+Open LAN Manager–network operating system
- ▶ 3+Open LAN Vision–network manager software
- ▶ EtherLink 16–high performance 16-bit Ethernet adapter
- ▶ EtherLink II–series of 8-bit Ethernet adapters
- ▶ EtherLink II/16–series of 16-bit ISA Ethernet adapters
- ▶ EtherLink III EISA–32-bit Ethernet adapter
- ▶ EtherLink III–parallel tasking 16-bit Ethernet adapter
- ▶ EtherLink III PCMCIA–credit card Ethernet adapter
- ▶ EtherLink Plus–16-bit intelligent Ethernet adapter
- ▶ EtherLink/MC–16-bit Microchannel Ethernet adapter
- ▶ EtherLink/MC32–32-bit Microchannel Ethernet adapter
- ▶ FDDILink–FDDI LAN interface boards
- ▶ FDDILink–series of 32-bit EISAS FDDI adapters
- ▶ ISOVIEW–network management software for OS/2
- ▶ LinkWatch–network management for Ethernet and token ring LANs
- ▶ Maxess/Windows–LAN-to-mainframe interface
- ▶ NETBuilder Basic–network protocol software
- ▶ NETBuilder II–network protocol software
- ▶ Netprobe–LAN management software
- ▶ PCS/TCP–TCP/IP software package
- ▶ TokenLink III ISA/EISA/MCA–token ring adapters

Voice Support, Standard
408-727-7021 or 800-876-3266

Online Computer Support

Computer Support via 3 Com's BBS: 408-980-8204

Computer Support via Internet ftp: ftp.3com.com

Worldwide Support
  Germany phone: 089-678210

20/20 Software

Voice, Standard Support: 503-520-0504

Fax Support: 503-520-9118

Online Computer Support

  CompuServe:
  Type: GO TWENTY to the third-party G+ forum
  in which we are a vendor. In our forum, we offer
  tech support, upgrades, and demo and sales
  literature.

AbleSoft

▶ Card Collector, The–sports card collector's
  database
▶ Comic Collector, The–collector
  database/inventory program
▶ Family for Windows–Windows software to track
  family history

Voice Support, Standard: 800-545-9009

Above Software, Inc.

▶ Above Disc–memory-management utility,
  emulates EMS
▶ 4.0 in extended memory
▶ Above Utilities for DOS–utility collection
▶ AboveLAN–LAN memory-management software
▶ AboveMEM–memory extender add-in for 1-2-3
  Release 2.*x*
▶ AboveX–information exchange package
▶ Golden Retriever–modified version of Ready, Aim,
  FILE!

Voice Support, Standard: 714-851-2283

Online Computer Support

   Online Support via Above's BBS: 714-851-5102

Abra Cadabra Software

- ▶ Abra 2000–computerized human resource system
- ▶ Abra 2000 Attendance Module
- ▶ AbraPay–payroll processing system
- ▶ AbraScan–OCR resume scanning module for AbraTrak
- ▶ AbraTrain–employee training management software
- ▶ AbraTrak–applicant tracking software
- ▶ Envoy Pay–Windows payroll software

Voice Support, Standard: 813-579-1111

Accent Software International

- ▶ Accent word processor
- ▶ Multilingual word processing packages for Windows
- ▶ Multilingual add-on utilities for existing Windows software

Voice, Standard Support: 800-535-5216
   Standard support is available 8 AM to 8 PM, Eastern Time, Monday to Friday. Installation support is free, followed by pay-per-period support.

Fax Support: 800-535-5257
   Fax support is primarily for registration and is available by fax-back service. Faxed questions will be acknowledged, and the customer will be invited to call in by telephone.

Accent Software International

Online Computer Support

CompuServe: 74774,264
Type: GO ACCENT
CompuServe section: Windows Vendor E Forum
(WINAPE), Section 17

Internet:
E-mail address: 74774.264@CompuServe.com

Worldwide Support

English: 44-923-208435

French: 44-923-208424 or in France, toll free
059-08242

German: 44 923 208436 or in Germany, toll free
0130-813906

Access Software, Inc.

▶ 10th Frame–pro bowling simulator
▶ Above Disc Plus
▶ Above Utilities for Windows
▶ Amazon: The Guardians of Eden–adventure game
▶ Cartel
▶ Countdown–interactive mystery game
▶ Crime Wave–adventure game
▶ Echelon–3D space flight simulator
▶ Echelon with Real Sound
▶ Famous Courses of the World, Vol I–III
▶ Heavy Metal–Modern Land Combat Vol I
▶ Links 386 Pro–interactive golf simulation game
▶ Links: Castle Pines Golf Club, Home of The
  International
▶ Links: Championship Courses
▶ Links: The Challenge of Golf–interactive golf
  simulation
▶ Links course disks (Banff Springs, Barton Creek
  Country Club, Bay Hill Club & Lodge, Bountiful

Golf Club, Copperhead at Innisbrook, Dorado Beach Puerto Rico, Firestone Country Club, Hyatt, Innisbrook, Mauna Kea, Pinehurst Country Club, The Belfry, Troon North)
- ▶ Lip Stik Plus
- ▶ Martian Memorandum–interactive fiction
- ▶ Mean Streets–interactive detective movie
- ▶ Triple Pack–includes Raid Over Moscow and Beach Head I & II
- ▶ Under A Killing Moon–interactive movie on CD-ROM
- ▶ World Class Leader Board

Voice, Standard Support: 800-793-8324
Standard support is available 7:30 AM to 8:20 PM, Central Time, Monday to Friday.

Fax Support: 801-359-2968

Online Computer Support

Computer Support via Access' BBS: 801-364-7449
This BBS has four lines, all supporting up to 14.4K.

CompuServe: 72662,61

America OnLine: Keyword: LINKSPRO1

Delphi: LINKSPRO1

Internet:
E-mail addresses: linkspro1@delphi.com, linkspro1@aol.com, or 72662.61@CompuServe.com

Acclaim Software, Inc.
- ▶ EditPro–Windows-based text editor

Voice, Standard Support: 619-452-3633

Accolade

▶ Gaming software

Voice, Standard Support: 408-296-8400
Standard support is available 8 AM to 5 PM, Pacific Time, Monday to Friday.

Fax Support: 408-246-0231

Online Computer Support

America OnLine: Keyword: ACCOLADE

CompuServe: 76004,2132
Type: GO GAMAPUB

Internet:
E-mail addresses: 76004.2132@CompuServe.com or accolade@aol.com

ACECAD

▶ Pens, slates, and keyboards

Voice, Standard Support: 408-655-9911
Standard support is available 8:30 AM to 5 PM, Pacific Time, Monday to Friday.

Fax Support: 408-655-1919
Support via ACECAD's fax is available 24 hours, Monday through Friday, not including national holidays. You should receive a reply the same day that you send your fax or the following work day.

Online Computer Support

Computer support via ACECAD's BBS: 408-655-1988

☎ Call the standard support number for information on how to contact ACECAD on CompuServe and America OnLine.

Acer America (ACROS)

▶ Computers and monitors

Voice, Standard Support: 800-251-2237
   Standard support is available 24 hours, 7 days a
   week, and is a lifetime service to customers with
   a validation number.

Fax Support via ACROS' BBS: 408-428-0140
   If you have a fax modem, you can get through
   the BBS and have service through ACROS'
   audimated voice faxback.

Online Computer Support

   Computer Support via ACER's BBS: 408-428-0140

   Internet:
   E-mail address: tsup@smtplink.altos.com

   CompuServe: Keyword: GO ACER

ACMA

▶ Desktop computers (486s and Pentiums)

Voice, Standard Support: 800-786-8998
   Standard support is available 8 AM to 5 PM, Pacific
   Time, Monday to Saturday.

Fax Support: 510-629-0629
   Be sure to include an invoice number or serial
   number when you fax in your problem.

Online Computer Support

   Computer Support via ACMA's BBS: 510-651-1606

☎ Call the standard support number for
   information regarding support via the Internet.

Actix Systems, Inc.

- ▶ GraphicsENGINE 1280TC–S3-based 1280×1024 graphics
- ▶ GraphicsENGINE 32VL–VL-bus graphics board with S3 processor
- ▶ GraphicsENGINE 32VL Plus–VL-bus graphics board w/S3 processor
- ▶ GraphicsENGINE 64 PCI–PCI local bus graphics board
- ▶ GraphicsENGINE Display Accelerator
- ▶ GraphicsENGINE VGA–high-resolution graphics accelerator board
- ▶ ProSTAR Series of Windows accelerators for local bus systems
- ▶ Quantum–SuperVGA Windows accelerator graphics card
- ▶ Spectrum series of 32,768 color VGA cards
- ▶ Tiger series of 1280×1024 high refresh rate display adapters

Voice Support, Standard: 408-986-1625

Online Computer Support

   Computer Support via BBS: 408-970-3719

Addtron Technology

- ▶ Local area network products
- ▶ Ethernet adapters, concentrators, and repeaters

Voice, Standard Support: 800-998-4646
   Standard support is available 8 AM to 5 PM, Pacific Time, Monday to Friday.

Fax Support: accessible by Addtron's BBS

Online Computer Support

   Computer Support via Addtron's BBS: 510-770-0272

☎ Other means of technical support for Addtron are found in their text files and manuals with their products.

Adobe/Aldus Systems

▶ PageMaker
▶ Persuasion
▶ Freehand and Photoshop
▶ Fetch
▶ Gallery Effects

Voice, Standard Support: 800-833-6687
More specific support numbers are available through this number. Standard support is available 7 AM to 5 PM, Pacific Time, Monday to Friday. If you buy a new retail product, you will receive 90 days of free technical support.

Voice, Priority Support: 900-555-2200
Priority support through this number is $2 per minute and is available 24 hours, Monday to Friday.

TT/TTD Support: 206-343-3381

Fax Support:
Support via fax is available to specific products by calling the standard support number.

Online Computer Support

Computer Support via Adobe's BBS: 206-623-6984

☎ For support via CompuServe and America OnLine, call standard support number for further information.

Advanced Graphics Software, Inc.

▶ Science Figure Pack–library accessory for SlideWrite
▶ Plus
▶ SlideWrite Plus–presentation graphics software
▶ SlideWrite Plus for Windows–presentation graphics software
▶ SlideWrite Presenter

Voice Support, Standard: 619-931-1919

Aetech, Inc.

▶ Ada Assembler
▶ Ada Software Development Toolset
▶ Ada Training Environment
▶ AdaGraphics–graphics toolkit for Ada programmers
▶ AdaScope Debugger
▶ IntegrAda–international standard ADA programming language
▶ IntegrAda for Windows–standard ADA programming language
▶ LearnAda–college level hands-on training course

Voice Support, Standard: 619-431-7714

AimTech Corp.

▶ IconAuthor
▶ CBT Express

Additional options are available for both priority support and extensions beyond the original free period.

Voice, Standard Support: 800-289-2884

Fax Support: 603-883-5582

Online Computer Support

Computer Support via AinTech's BBS: 603-598-8402

CompuServe: 75300,2430
Type: GO AIMTECH (Ultimedia Tools Series
Forum) or GO MULTIVEN (Multimedia Vendors
Forum, AimTech Section)

Internet:
E-mail address: support@aimtech.com

AlarmPro/Alarm Clock

▶ AlarmPro
▶ Alarm Clock

Voice, Standard Support: 901-683-3770
Standard support is available after 6 PM, Central
Time.

Online Computer Support

CompuServe: 70304,2705

Internet: 70304.2705@CompuServe.com.

Aldus Corp.

▶ Advanced Aldus Classroom: Designing with
PageMaker–training
▶ ChartMaker–incorporate charts in any application
▶ FreeHand–graphics design and illustration
software
▶ Gallery Effects: Classic Art, Vol 1 & 2–for Windows
▶ Gallery Effects: Texture Art–for Windows
▶ PageMaker Classroom–training package
▶ TrapWise for Windows–spot and process color
trapping

- ▶ InfoPublisher Database Addition
- ▶ IntelliDraw–intelligent drawing program for Windows
- ▶ PageMaker–desktop publisher
- ▶ PageMaker for Windows–page layout/desktop publishing software
- ▶ PageMaker Portfolio: Designs for Business Communications
- ▶ PageMaker Portfolio: Designs for Manuals–templates
- ▶ PageMaker Portfolio: Designs for Newsletters–templates
- ▶ Persuasion–Windows presentation software
- ▶ PhotoStyler–full color image processing software (U-Lead Sys)
- ▶ Snapshot
- ▶ TypeTwister for Windows–text editing utility

Technical support: See Adobe

Allegro New Media

- ▶ CD-ROM
- ▶ PCs Library
- ▶ Business 500 Multimedia
- ▶ Learn-To-Do Windows & Desktop Publishing
- ▶ Clinton Health Security Plan

Voice, Standard Support: 201-808-1992
   Standard support is available 8:30 AM to 5:30 PM, Eastern Time, Monday to Friday.

Fax Support: 201-808-2645

Online Computer Support

   America OnLine: Keyword: GO BUREADEV

   CompuServe: 71332,2645

Alpha Software Corporation

- ▶ Alpha Database
- ▶ Alpha Four version 4.0.11 (DOS)
- ▶ Alpha Five for Windows
- ▶ Bravo!, version 3 (Windows)

Voice, Standard Support: 617-272-3680
> Standard support is free for the first 60 days, after which users must purchase a support plan.

Voice, Priority Support: 900-555-ALPH
> This 900 number is pay-per-use, with the first minute free, followed by $2 per minute.

Fax Support: 617-273-1507

Online Computer Support

> *Computer Support via Alpha's BBS:* 617-229-2915
>
> *America OnLine:* Keyword: GO ALPHATECH
>
> *Prodigy:* Jump to COMPUTER SUPPORT BB
>
> *CompuServe:* 75300,3656

ALR

- ▶ Evolution and Revolution series of machines
- ▶ PCs

Voice, Standard Support: 800-257-1230
> Standard support is available 6 AM to 6 PM, Pacific Time, Monday to Friday.

Fax Support: 714-458-0532
> Faxback service also is available by touch tone phone: 714-581-3332.

Online Computer Support

> *Computer Support by ALR's BBS:* 714-458-6834
>
> *CompuServe:* Keyword: GO ALR,INC.

☎ ALR also has technical support through their foreign offices.

Altima

▶ Laptops

Voice, Standard Support: 510-356-5600

Fax Support: 510-356-2408
   This fax collects calls 24 hours.

Online Computer Support

   Computer Support via Altima's BBS: 510-603-2753

Amaze, Inc.

▶ Cathy Computer Calendar, The–page-a-day calendar software
▶ Far Side Computer Calendar, The–page-a-day calendar software
▶ Far Side Daily Planner for Windows, The
▶ Trivial Pursuit Daily Planner
▶ Trivial Pursuit Daily Planner: Sports Edition

Voice Support, Standard: 206-820-7007

Ambra Computer Corp.

▶ Notebooks and subnotebooks
▶ Desktop minitowers
▶ Pentium systems (P60–90)

Voice, Standard Support: 800-465-2227
   Standard support is available on a 24-hour basis.

Online Computer Support

   Computer support via Ambra's BBS: 905-316-7952

A

American Cybernetics, Inc.

Voice, Standard Support: 602-968-1945
Standard support is available 9 AM to 4 PM,
Central Time, Monday to Friday. All calls are
answered promptly (users don't have to spend
time on hold to get a technician).

Fax Support: 602-966-1654

Online Computer Support

CompuServe: 71333,10
Keyword: GO CYBERNET. Choose section 11
(American Cybernet). American Cybernetics also
posts patches and bugs fixes in their forum's
library. They also accept direct CompuServe
E-mail if users don't want to post their message
to a public forum. Messages on CompuServe
usually are responded to by the next working
day (i.e., message posted on Thursday afternoon
would be answered by the end of Friday).

Internet:
E-mail address: tech@amcyber.com

Special Information

American Cybernetics also routinely checks the
newsgroup comp.editors for any questions that
are related to their products. American
Cybernetics plans to add both an FTP site and an
American Cybernetics newsgroup in the near
future. Messages sent via E-mail on the Internet
usually are responded to by the next working day.
Questions posed in the newsgroup comp.editors
usually are answered within two days.

American Laser Games

Voice, Standard Support: 505-837-5400 or
    505-837-5416

Fax Support: 505-880-1557

Online Computer Support

CompuServe: 74774,773
They also have two vendor forums: GO VIDPUB,
Section 12 and GO GAMDPUB, Section 14.

Prodigy: Post a note on the CD games forum, and
they will answer it.

Ami Pro

▶ Spreadsheets
▶ Word processors
▶ Graphics pack
▶ Personal information manager
▶ Databases

Voice, Standard Support

DOS, MacIntosh: 508-988-6400
OS/2: 508-988-2820
Windows: 508-988-2500
(expired technical assistance: 900-555-6887)
Standard support is available 8 AM to 8 PM,
Eastern Time, Monday to Friday.

TT/TDD Support

800-457-0909 (U.S.A.)
800-563-1109 (Canada)
404-698-7663 (world)
For TT/TDD Support, you must have a telecom
dial-direct terminal.

Voice, Priority Support: Pay-for-service
You can purchase unlimited access for one year.
You also can pay per instance by paying a one-
time fee for the same problem.

Fax Support: 617-693-7000

Online Computer Support

☎ Computer support via AmiPro's BBS is accessible
through CompuServe. There are five different
forums off CompuServe, one of which deals
exclusively with technical support.

Special Information
You can order direct membership to AmiPro's
technical support by calling 800-967-7200.

AMS

▶ Notebooks and portables

Voice, Standard Support: 800-886-3536 or
818-813-2391
Standard support is available 6 AM to 6 PM, Pacific
Time, Monday through Friday, and 9 AM to 3 PM,
Saturday.

Fax Support: 818-813-2381

Online Computer Support

Computer Support via AMS' BBS: 818-813-2383 or
818-813-2384

Special Information
Technical support videos by AMS for Windows
and DOS will be available soon.

Amtex Software Corp.

Voice, Standard Support: 613-967-7900
Technical support at Amtex is free of charge to all registered users of Tristan, Eight Ball Deluxe, Gone Fishin', Royal Flush, SALS, and Sail Simulator.

Fax Support: 613-967-7902

Online Computer Support

Computer Support via Amtex's BBS: 613-967-9789

CompuServe: 74774,142

Internet: info@amtex.com

Animotion Development Inc.

▶ MCS CDMaster–CD player with database
▶ MCS Stereo–CD, MIDI, and wave player, also includes wave editor, wave recorder, and mixing console
▶ MCS SoundTrak–An enhanced wave editor with Q-Sound functionality
▶ MCS SoundSavers–screen savers that respond to the sounds going through your sound card
▶ MCS Sound Revue–An enhanced wave editor with 300 sound effects included on CD ROM

Voice, Standard Support: 205-591-5715

Fax Support: 205-591-5716

Online Computer Support

Computer Support via Animotion's BBS: 205-591-5795

CompuServe: GO ANIMOTION

Apexx Tech

▶ PC networking products for connecting PCs to one another, as well as PCs to MacIntoshes

Voice, Standard Support: 208-336-9400
Standard support is available 8 AM to 6 PM,
Central Time, Monday to Friday.

Fax Support: 208-336-9445

Online Computer Support

CompuServe: 71043,2403

Apogee

Voice, Standard Support: 214-278-5655
Standard support is available 8 AM to 6 PM,
Central Time, Monday to Friday.

Fax Support: 214-278-4670

Online Computer Support

Computer Support via Apogee's BBS: 508-368-7036
This number will put you in direct contact with
Software Creations, the Apogee BBS. Software
Creations is Apogee's #1 file site. Apogee's games
are released there before anywhere else in the
world, so if you want the latest stuff, take a trip
over to Software Creations.

There are several BBS networks that are
monitored for Apogee messages. Apogee online
support representatives monitor all of the
following BBS networks: Fidonet, Relaynet
(Rime), Intelec, Ilink, U'NI-Net, and Smartnet.
All of these BBS networks have games,
shareware, and Apogee conferences.

Fidonet: 1:124/9006
Rime: APOGEE (or 1674)

Apogee also has a FDN on the Fidonet Filebone.
Check with your local Fidonet Filebone
administration for more info on how to get
Apogee's shareware delivered right to your BBS!

Apogee

Check FILEBONE.NA (available from your local Fidonet administration) for more information.

Internet:
E-mail address: apogee@metronet.com or joe.siegler@swcbbs.com

Apogee also has a mailing list on the Internet, where they send press releases, general Apogee information, new game release notifications, and other miscellaneous items out on. Drop Apogee a line at one of the previous Internet addresses, and they'll put you on. Just say the word!

Apogee also has a "finger" plan set up for the most up-to-date online information about Apogee software. Finger apogee@fohnix.metronet.com for the most up-to-the-second information about our releases! If you are unsure of whether you can do this or if you don't know what "finger" access is, please check with your local Internet service provider for more information on this Internet service.

Apogee has an official FTP site for our shareware episodes. The latest stuff is always available for anonymous FTP by FTPing to ftp.uml.edu in the directory msdos/Games/Apogee.

CompuServe: 74200,553

America Online: Keyword: APOGEE

GEnie: APOGEE

Prodigy: CXVP94A

See the appropriate instructions for these various services on how to send private mail to these addresses. All of these services have Internet E-mail gateways, but please, if you're sending Internet E-mail, use the swcbbs.com address.

Apogee

Special Information

Apogee asks that you please be at your computer and have it ready for assistance when contacting their technical support. If you can't be at your computer, please have printouts of the following things available, so that they may assist you better. It might be possible to provide technical support without these things, but it will be much more difficult.

The needed files are CONFIG.SYS and AUTOEXEC.BAT, plus a description of what happens when you execute the MEM /C command (or just MEM if you get an error using MEM /C).

Apple Computers, Inc.

Voice, Standard Support: 800-757-2775 or 800-950-2442
Standard support is available 6 AM to 6 PM, Pacific Time, Monday through Friday. (Hours of available support may vary according to Apple product.)

Priority Support: 800-745-2775 or 800-950-2442

Automated/Fax Support: 800-505-0171

TTD Support: 800-776-2333 or 800-833-6223 (TTY)
The Macintosh Disability Resources packet (MDR) provides information on adaptive hardware and software products and solutions that make Apple technology accessible to individuals with a disability.

Online Computer Support

Internet: ftp.austin.apple.com
www.info.apple.com

E-World: 800-775-4556

Apple Customer Center, Quick Answer Area

AppleLink: 800-877-8221
Support Area

CompuServe: 800-848-8990
Apple Support Forum, Apple Tech Info Library

Special Information

If you have a question about software, you often can find an answer by clicking the Balloon Help icon at the upper-right corner of the menu bar on your screen and choosing Show Balloons.

Authorized Apple Resellers can provide software support, guidance, and technical consulting services. Many resellers also are Apple Authorized Service Providers and can provide hardware repair services. Apple supplies Authorized Service Providers with the tools, information, and technical backup that they need to assist you. To locate an Authorized Apple Reseller, call 800-538-9696, ext. 525.

As Apple does not provide support for non-Apple software programs, your questions are best directed to the manufacturer for the application program that you're using. The phone number for assistance generally is listed in the front of the program reference manual.

Approach Software Corp.

Voice Support, Standard: 415-306-0646

Online Computer Support

Computer Support via Approach's BBS: 415-368-5390

CompuServe: 76646,3367

Internet: help@approach.com

Arcadia Technologies, Inc.

Voice, Standard Support: 818-446-6945

Fax Support: 818-447-4212

Online Computer Support

   Computer Support via Arcadia's BBS: 818-447-8289

   CompuServe: 72662,1042

   Internet:
   E-mail address: 72662,1042@compuserve.com

Artisoft

Voice, Standard Support: 602-670-7000
   Standard support is available 7 AM to 5 PM,
   Central Time, Monday to Friday

Fax Support: 602-884-8665

Fax Retreival System: 602-884-1397 (tech
   support bulletins)

Online Computer Support

   Computer Support via Artisoft's BBS: 602-884-8648
   (1200–9600) or 602-884-9675 (14.4K)

   TTY machine: 602-670-7352

   CompuServe: Type: GO ARTISOFT

☎ Note: CIS and BBS are for timely, noncritical
   questions/answers.

   Priority Support: 900-555-8324 ($2.50 per minute)
   or 800-293-3936 ($2.50 per minute)
   Fee-based services are available 6 AM to 6 PM,
   Central Time, Monday to Friday, and 6 AM to
   5 PM, Central Time, Saturday. They are payable
   by Master Card, VISA, and American Express.

Artist Graphics, Inc.

Voice Support, Standard: 612-631-7800

Fax On Demand Support: 612-631-3509

Online Computer Support

> *Voice Support via Artist Graphics' BBS:*
> 612-631-7664

> *Internet:* agteca@csinc.mn.org

Ashlar Inc.

Voice, Standard Support: 800-966-2348 or
408-746-1800

> Standard support is available 6 AM to 5 PM,
> Pacific Time, Monday to Friday.

Fax Support: 408-746-0749

Online Computer Support

> *CompuServe:* 71333,1060
> Section (#8) in the CADDVEN forum

> *AppleLink:* GO VELLUM

Ask Me Multimedia

► Guide To Multimedia CD-ROM
► Multimedia Library CD-ROM
► Super Show & Tell

Voice, Standard Support: 612-531-0603 or
800-275-0645

> Standard support is available 8:30 AM to 5:30 PM,
> Central Time, Monday to Friday.

Fax Support: 612-531-0645

> Fax in a description of your problem along with
> any pertinent information and Multimedia will
> either call or fax you back.

Online Computer Support

Computer Support via Multimedia's BBS:
612-531-0702

Ask Sam Systems

- ▶ Ask Sam Lan
- ▶ Ask Sam For Windows
- ▶ Ask Sam For Dos
- ▶ Free-Form Data Base Systems

Voice, Standard Support: 904-584-6590
Support is available 9 AM to 6 PM, Eastern Time,
Monday through Friday.

Fax Support: 904-584-7481

Online Computer Support

Computer Support via Ask Sam System's BBS:
904-584-8287

CompuServe: 74774,352
Keyword GO ASKSAM

AST Research

- ▶ Hardware computer systems
- ▶ Support software preinstalled in shipment

Voice, Standard Support: 800-727-1278
Standard support is available 24 hours, 7 days a
week.

Fax Support: 800-926-1278

Online Computer Support

Computer Support via AST's BBS: 714-727-4723 or
714-727-4132

CompuServe: Keyword: GO AST

Prodigy: Jump to AST SUPPORT

Worldwide Support
Ontario: 905-507-3278

Beijing: 86-1-505-2950

U.K., Europe: 44-81-2325000

Australia: 61-2-415-5400

Hong Kong: 852-806-4333

ATI Technologies, Inc.

- ▶ 14400 ETC-EXPRESS V.32bis PCMCIA fax modem
- ▶ 19200 ETC-E 19.2kbps V32terbo data modem
- ▶ 2400 FAX-ETC internal fax/data modem
- ▶ 2400etc/i Internal Modem Card
- ▶ 2400etc/i+SendFAX–internal modem/fax board
- ▶ 8514-Vantage–8514/A Graphics Board
- ▶ 8514/ULTRA graphics board
- ▶ 9600etc/e 9600bps external modem
- ▶ Audio FX–stereo sound board
- ▶ CD Sound Dimension Multimedia Upgrade Kit
- ▶ Graphics Pro Turbo–graphics accelerator board
- ▶ Graphics Solution–multipurpose mono-color graphics card
- ▶ Graphics Ultra
- ▶ Graphics Ultra Plus–1280×1024 256-color graphics board
- ▶ Graphics Ultra Pro–Windows/CAD/multimedia graphics board
- ▶ Graphics Ultra Pro EISA–multimedia graphics board
- ▶ Graphics Ultra Pro VLB–VL-bus multimedia graphics board
- ▶ Graphics Ultra+ graphics accelerator board
- ▶ Graphics Vantage–combined coprocessor & SuperVGA graphics
- ▶ Graphics Wonder–MACH 32 graphics accelerator card

ATI Technologies, Inc.

- ▶ Graphics Xpression Mach 64 graphics card
- ▶ MediaMerge–video editing program
- ▶ Messenger–multifunction communications board
- ▶ Stereo F/X–stereo sound board
- ▶ VGA Integra–enhanced VGA graphics card
- ▶ VGABasic-16 graphics board
- ▶ VGAStereo F/X–VGA graphics board with sound interface
- ▶ VGAudio FX–VGA Wonder video board with stereo sound
- ▶ VGAWonder Turbo–graphics & video accelerator board
- ▶ VGAWonder Video Card
- ▶ VGAWonder XL–1024×768 SuperVGA graphics board
- ▶ Video Wonder–full-motion video & graphics brd
- ▶ Video-It!–low-cost, high-performance video capture card
- ▶ WinTurbo–graphics accelerator board

Voice, Standard Support: 905-882-2626
Standard support is available 9 AM to 7 PM, Eastern Time, Monday to Friday.

Fax Support: 905-882-0546

Online Computer Support

Computer Support by ATI's BBS: 905-764-9404

CompuServe: 74740,667

Internet: ATITECH.CA
E-mail address: 74740.667@compuserv.com

Special Information
Other sources for technical assistance are the troubleshooting guides that are found inside each product's manual. Also, it might be of interest to you that, on CompuServe and the

ATI Technologies, Inc.

Internet, you can talk to other users about technical assistance and might find answers without having to make direct contact with your product's support system.

Autodesk, Inc.

- ▶ 3D Studio–high-end 3D animation software
- ▶ Animation Player for Visual Basic
- ▶ Animation Player for Windows
- ▶ Animator–interactive desktop video
- ▶ Animator Pro–animation software with added SuperVGA support
- ▶ AutoCAD
- ▶ AutoCAD AEC Architectural
- ▶ AutoCAD for Windows
- ▶ AutoConvert
- ▶ Autodesk 3D Concepts
- ▶ Autodesk Multimedia Explorer
- ▶ AutoShade–AutoCAD companion rendering program
- ▶ AutoSketch–entry-level drafting software
- ▶ AutoSolid
- ▶ AutoVision–control light and surface effects in AutoCAD
- ▶ CADD Starter Kit
- ▶ Cyberspace Developer Kit (CDK)–3D visualization tool
- ▶ DeskConvert
- ▶ DotPlot
- ▶ EGA Extender
- ▶ Estimator
- ▶ GenCADD Architectural 1–CAD package for architectural use
- ▶ Generic 3D Drafting
- ▶ Generic 3D Solids

- ▶ Generic CADD Levels 1-3
- ▶ Generic CADD Starter Kit
- ▶ Generic Presentation
- ▶ Generic Utilities–import utility for Generic CADD
- ▶ Graphic Impact–Windows-based presentation package
- ▶ Home Series: 3D Plan
- ▶ Home Series: Bathroom
- ▶ Home Series: Deck
- ▶ Home Series: Home
- ▶ Home Series: Kitchen
- ▶ Home Series: Landscape
- ▶ HyperChem–complex chemistry in Windows
- ▶ IGES
- ▶ Instant Artist–simplified desktop publishing software
- ▶ James Gleick's CHAOS: The Software
- ▶ Office Layout–design and plan office and facility space
- ▶ Org Plus for Windows–organization charts
- ▶ PenPlot
- ▶ Rudy Rucker Cellular Automata Laboratory (CL Lab)
- ▶ Symbols Library: Geometric Positioning
- ▶ Symbols Library: Residential Framing Details
- ▶ Symbols Library: Welding

Voice Support, Standard: 206-487-2934 or 800-538-6401

Standard support is available 6 AM to 5 PM, Pacific Time, Monday to Friday. This support is free; however, extended consulting service is priced through dealers. For specific prices, call customer service and contact your nearest dealer.

Autodesk, Inc.

Fax On Demand Support: 707-794-1444

Online Computer Support

> *Computer Support via Autodesk's BBS:* 415-289-2270
> Available at Autodesk Global Village on the BBS
>
> *CompuServe:* Type: GO ACAD

☎ Technical support also is available on dealer channels and the customer service phone line: 800-538-6401.

Automap

▶ Automap Streets
▶ Automap Pre
▶ Am Road Atlas For DOS, Macintosh, and Windows

Voice, Standard Support: 206-455-3552, ext. 128
Standard support is available 8:30 AM to 5 PM, Pacific Time, Monday to Friday.

Fax Support: 206-455-3667

Mark Cabey of Avalon Hill

▶ Kingmaker (PCs), Operation Crusader (PCs and Mac)

As a support technician for Avalon Hill, Mark Cabey tries to help his customers solve their hardware and software problems so that they can get their computer games up and running. He answers direct telephone calls, letters, and E-mail messages via the online services.

"The best feeling I know," says Cabey, "is when my customer hangs up the phone playing our game without any problems." He says that it actually is kind of fun to try and troubleshoot someone else's system from the root of their problem. "As I am helping someone through a problem, I am learning more myself, as well."

The "know-it-all" customer is Cabey's least favorite aspect of his job. "Once in a while I will receive a caller who thinks he or she knows it all and that the problem

Online Computer Support

Computer Support via Automap's BBS: 206-646-9130

CompuServe: Keyword: GO AUTOMAP

Internet:
Support varies for each individual product. Look under "AUTOMAP" logo for complete listing.

E-world: AUTOMAP

☎ Automap also provides technical support through registration cards and personal mail.

Avalon Hill

▶ Kingmaker (PCs)
▶ Operation Crusader (PCs and Macs)

Voice, Standard Support: 410-426-9600

Fax Support: 410-254-0991

---

is the software and not their hardware. 'It couldn't be my computer, no way!' they say."

Most of Cabey's computer background was derived from what he learned in college as a Computer Information Systems major. He successfully completed six computer language courses (COBOL, RPG, FORTRAN, GW-BASIC, QBASIC, and Object Oriented++). He also worked at Electronics Boutique for over a year, where he made his computer contacts.

Cabey came to Avalon Hill through the job bank at his college and ended up switching from a full-time student/part-time computer retailer to a full-time computer support person who goes to class at night. He is a college senior and should have his bachelor's degree in CIS by fall 1995.

Cabey says that the most difficult question that he has encountered probably is one he received his first day on the job at Avalon. In fact, it was literally the first ques-

Continued . . .

Online Computer Support

CompuServe:
Avalon Hill Computer Games: 72662,1207
Avalon Hill Board Games: 72662,2443

America OnLine:
Avalon Hill Computer Games: AH GAMES

GEnie:
Avalon Hill Computer Games: AVALON.HILL
Avalon Hill Board Games: AVALON.HILL2

Avery

▶ Avery LabelPro Windows
▶ LabelPro Laser
▶ LabelPro Dot Matrix
▶ Mac LabelPro and various templates and formatting disks

Voice, Standard Support: 214-776-2699
Standard support is available 8 AM to 8 PM, Eastern Time, Monday to Friday.

tion he received from his first caller. "I didn't have a vast knowledge of the games here, and it's tough to solve a problem without a 'particular' knowledge." Cabey told the caller he'd get back to him, proceeded to consult one of Avalon's "military game experts," and called back with the lowdown. "I then was able to solve the problem."

The most frequently asked question, according to Cabey, is how to get more memory out of a system. Most people don't realize that, as more and more features are added into a game, the memory requirements go up, he says. "People believe that the amount of RAM that they have should be enough to run every game for a long time. But we all know that's not the case!" says Cabey. "Some people believe that having 4MB of RAM is enough, but 8MB of RAM is definitely becoming the standard for most games."

As for what callers can do to help Cabey arrive at a solution for them, he says the callers should always be in

Priority Support: 800-541-5507

    Avery offers Avery Support Plus, which provides an 800 number with priority access to support technicians and free Avery supplies.

Fax Support: 214-776-2400

FaxFacts Information Service: 818-584-1681

    This fax offers a 24-hour service where clients can receive information on how to print Avery labels with a variety of software packages.

Online Computer Support

    CompuServe: Type: GO AVERY

Axik Computers

▶ PCs, Work Station, File Server
▶ Net Power Enterprise File Server series
▶ Ace Cashe 486 series
▶ Ace Power 586 series
▶ Ace Cashe 486vg2 Cutless

front of their computer, know what kind of computer they own, what the exact problem is that they are encountering, and know what their computer consists of (what kind of sound card, what kind of video card, etc.). "When the person calling knows most, if not all, of these items, their problem usually can be solved in a matter of minutes," says Cabey.

To solve problems on their own, Cabey gives computer users the golden rule: "Read, read, then read some more. That's how all computer professionals learn and stay up with the times. We read manuals and textbooks and listen to other computer professionals."

Specifically, Cabey advises users to read thoroughly the troubleshooting guides that accompany computer software. He says that 9 out of 10 problems can be solved using these guides and that most calls are solved by tech people using these guides. So why not cut to the chase and use them yourself.

- ▶ Word Perfect Authorized Educational Reseller
- ▶ MicroSoft Authorized Educational Reseller
- ▶ Acer Authorized Reseller
- ▶ Compaq Authorized Reseller
- ▶ IBM Authorized Reseller

Voice, Standard Support: 800-724-1223 or
716-223-2300

Standard support is available 8 AM to 5 PM,
Monday through Friday. Support agreements
can be hourly or prepaid for blocks of hours
(minimum 40 hours). After business hour support
by pager available at extra charge (double time
in off hours). No free support available.

Fax Support: 716-223-3484

Online Computer Support

CompuServe: 76077,2655

E-mail: lee+ra+azatar%azatar@mcimail.com

Bill Kalegeros of Axik Computer, Inc.

- ▶ PCs, Work Station, File Server, Net Power Enterprise
file server series, Ace Cache 486 series, Ace Power
586 series, Ace Cache 486vg2 Cutlass

"People are starting to treat the computer as another
form of consumer product such as television," says Bill
Kalegeros, a computer support technician with Axik
Computer, Inc. He has been in the computer industry
for 11 years, starting with a major Japanese company
selling CPM-based PCs and dedicated word-processing
systems. At that time, says Kalegeros, a word processor
with "advanced" technology was a steal at $14,000. A
sales management position with a large service company handling support for Axik Computer steered him
inside the Axik company. Kalegeros says his reason for
changing jobs was the fine quality of systems that were
being produced by Axik, which was shipping systems at
a less than 1% FFR (Field Failure Rate).

Voice, Standard Support: 408-735-1234,
   ext. 121 or ext. 116
   Standard support is available 8 AM to 5 PM, Pacific
   Time, Monday to Friday, and 10 AM to 4 PM,
   Saturday.

Fax Support: 408-735-1437
   Fax in a detailed description of your problem,
   and you will be faxed back an answer within
   two hours.

☎ Call the standard support number for
   information regarding support via the Internet
   and CompuServe.

Azatar MicroSystems

▶ Novell Gold Authorized Reseller
▶ DataEase Certified Consulting organization
▶ Novell Authorized Service Center
▶ Symantec Authorized Educational Reseller

As for the most difficult question Kalegeros has encountered, he says one of his customers called after their system had been run over by a forklift and wanted to know if it was covered under warranty. For the more typical problems, Kalegeros says that the most difficult situations are when a customer's system is not up and running and he must focus solely on getting them back up.

The most common questions Kalegeros hears from new users is "Where is the ANY key?" For more experienced users, he says their questions are more along the lines of multimedia situations, such as getting their CD to mount properly or compatibility issues with wavetable drivers with their sound card.

Kalegeros says that users can help him solve their problems more efficiently by reading the manual and checking the troubleshooting guide before calling him. "Also," he says, "computer users, especially new com-

Continued . . .

Special Information

1995 normal rates will be $80/hour ($70/hour prepaid), minimum 15-minute increments, double time on off hours and weekends. Travel time is charged portal to portal plus expenses if out of the immediate Rochester, NY area. Overnight travel is charged at $800/day plus expenses. Azatar has offices in Rochester, NY and in Syracuse, NY and serves the upstate NY area bordered by Rochester and Corning in the west and Syracuse and Binghamton in the east.

Azatar is the premier source for DataEase and Novell integration and optimization support.

puter users, need to explain exactly what they did to get the system to crash when it did and to be honest about it. We're not going to send them to their room without dinner or something."

As for what computer users can do to educate themselves, Kalegeros has one suggestion: read. "Read the computer magazines and weeklies, such as *Computer Currents* and *Microtimes*." He also suggests taking classes.

"If users become educated by reading and asking questions of their friends who already are using computers, it definitely will help," he says. "Both new and old users should not be afraid to get inside their systems. It really isn't as complicated as it looks."

B

Banner

Voice, Standard Support: 510-794-6850

Fax Support: 510-795-4488
Standard support is free to registered users.

Online Computer Support

CompuServe: Keyword: GO BANNER

Banyan Systems

▶ Banyan Vines (networking software)
▶ ENS
▶ Beyond Mail

Voice, Standard Support: Technical support is
available only through subscription.
"Banyan Knowledge Base" is a monthly support
subscription that costs $2,500 per year. Support
service with an onsite technician is $200,000 per
year. Emergency technical support is $1,895 per
year. Suscriptions are not sold directly and must
be purchased through a reseller.

Online Computer Support

Computer Support via Banyan's BBS: 508-836-1834

Internet: 130.86.90.1
When logging on, you have an anonymous
logon and your Internet address is the password.

BayWare, Inc.

▶ Software
▶ Power Japanese Version 2.0

Voice, Standard Support: 415-286-4488
Standard support is available 9 AM to 5 PM, Pacific
Time, Monday to Friday.

Fax Support: 415-578-1884
Be sure to put your fax to the attention of the technical department.

Beacon Software, Inc.

▶ Beacon Contact Management
▶ Family Genealogy
▶ MenuEase
▶ Price Sheet Quotation System
▶ SearchUtility

Voice, Standard Support: 419-242-3888 or 800-753-2322

Fax Support: 419-242-8247

Beame & Whiteside

▶ Network Compactivity Products, TCPIP Products
▶ Nfs, Multiconnect Products

Voice, Standard Support: 919-831-8975
Standard support is available 8 AM to 8 PM, Eastern Time, Monday to Friday. Every client has 45 days of free technical support. All evaluations have unlimited access to technical assistance as well as priority support.

Voice, Priority Support:
You can arrange priority support with a surcharge. Standard service gives access to priority support with free upgrades to products. The cost of priority service is 15% of a product's cost and is renewable on an annual basis.

Fax Support: 919-831-8990
Fax in a detailed description of your problem, and Beame & Whiteside will fax, call, or E-mail you back. The fax line also is available for international support.

Online Computer Support

Computer Support via Beame & Whiteside's BBS:
919-824-8160

STP Site: STP.BWS.com
You can download files at this site.

Internet: E-mail address: SUPPORT@bws.com

Berkeley Systems

Voice, Standard Support: 510-549-2300 or
510-549-2300, ext. 263

Fax Support: 510-849-9426

Online Computer Support

CompuServe: 75300,1375

America OnLine: PCstech@berksys.com

Best Data Products, Inc.

▶ ACE 5000
▶ 2842F/FX–28.8K modem and 14.4K fax.

Voice, Standard Support: 818-773-9600
Standard support is available 8 AM to 5 PM, Pacific
Time, Monday to Friday.

Fax Support: 818-773-9619

Online Computer Support

Computer Support via Best Data's BBS:
818-773-9627
This BBS has a message area, as well as on
CompuServe, in the Modem Vendor forum
(section 15).

CompuServe: via Best Data's BBS

Special Information
Best Data is a hardware manufacturer. The software that they provide with every one of their products comes from an outside developer (mainly Smith Micro).

Best Programs, Inc.

- ▶ Complete Pay
- ▶ FAS (Fixed Asset System)
- ▶ FAS for Windows
- ▶ Professional Tax Partner

Voice, Standard Support: 703-709-5200 or 800-368-2405

Fax Support: 703-709-9359

Best!Ware, Inc.

- ▶ Bestbooks–small business bookkeeping software for Windows
- ▶ M.Y.O.B.–small business accounting package
- ▶ M.Y.O.B. for Windows–small business accounting package

Voice, Standard Support: 201-586-2269 or 800-322-MYOB

Fax Support: 201-586-1553
Technical support information is faxed back automatically.

Bethesda Softworks

- ▶ Educational/recreational software
- ▶ The Elder Scrolls: ARENA
- ▶ Terminator: Rampage, Delta V, and T2029–arcade-style games
- ▶ Basketball Sim: NCAA2

B

Voice, Standard Support: 301-926-8300
  Standard support is available 11 AM to 5 PM,
  Eastern Time, Monday to Friday.

Hint Line: 900-963-Hints

Fax Support: 301-963-2000 (option #3)

Online Computer Support

  Computer Support via Bethesda Software's BBS: 301-
  990-7552

  CompuServe: 7133,234
  Type: GAMAPUB, Section 10

  America OnLine:
  Go word: BETHESDA
  E-mail: BETHESDA01

  Prodigy:
  E-mail address: BJSY29B

  GEnie:
  Category 8 on Scorpia's Round Table.
  E-mail: Bethesda

  Internet:
  E-mail only: Bethesda01@aol.com
  71333,234@compuserve.com

Big Noise Software, Inc.

Voice, Standard Support: 904-730-0754

Fax Support: 904-730-0748

Online Computer Support

  CompuServe: 75300,2470
  Support is in the MIDI A VENDOR forum,
  section 8.

Binar Graphics

- ▶ AnyView Utility–changes Windows video resolution
- ▶ Fantastic Recall
- ▶ SkyScraper Desktop Manager for OS/2
- ▶ WinSpeed–software-only graphics accelerator

Voice, Standard Support: 415-492-8161
Standard support is available 7 AM to 4 PM, Pacific Time, Monday to Friday.

Fax Support: 415-491-1164
Fax in a problem report with text files and copies of your system.

Online Computer Support

Computer Support via Binar's BBS: 415-491-0548

CompuServe: 73232,342

America OnLine: Keyword: GO BGTECH

Internet: binar@CRL.com

BIT Software, Inc.

- ▶ BitCom Deluxe–communications software
- ▶ BitFax Software for SendFax modems
- ▶ BitFax Easy Fax Software for Windows
- ▶ BitFax for Windows
- ▶ BitFax Professional for Windows
- ▶ BitFax/OCR for Windows
- ▶ FormManager II Database Management System

Voice, Standard Support: 510-490-2928

Fax Support: 510-490-9490

Online Computer Support

Computer Support via BIT Software's BBS Phone: 510-490-6637

B

Worldwide Support
Taipei, Taiwan
    Voice, Standard Support: 27855932
    Fax Support: 27855932

Bitstream, Inc.

- ► Bitstream PostScript Font Pack for Windows
- ► Bitstream Scaleable Typeface Packages
- ► Bitstream TrueType Font Packs for Windows
- ► Bitstream Type Essentials
- ► Bitstream Typeface Library in PostScript Type 1 format
- ► Bitstream Typeface Library in TrueType format for Windows
- ► Central Park Font Collection
- ► FaceLift for MS Windows
- ► FaceLift for WordPerfect
- ► FaceLift for WordPerfect Bonus Pack
- ► FaceLift Valuepack
- ► Fontware 3.0 for Windows
- ► Fontware 3.0 Starter Kit for Aldus PageMaker 3.0
- ► Fontware Installation Kits
- ► Fundamentals Packaged Typefaces
- ► Li'l Bits: The Flintstones Font Pack
- ► Li'l Bits: The Star Trek Font Pack
- ► Li'l Bits: The Winter Holiday Font Pack
- ► MakeUp for Windows
- ► MakeUp Soft Bundle
- ► Mosaic Printer Server Software for NetWare
- ► Skyscraper
- ► SoHo
- ► Type City Expandable LaserJet Font Cartridge

Voice, Standard Support: 617-497-7514

Worldwide Support

France

    Voice, Standard Support: 80241600

    Fax Support: 80240770

Bitware Australia Pty. Ltd.

▶ Galleria for OS/2, Version 2.1

Fax Support: 61-6-2810175

Online Computer Support

    CompuServe: 100033,340

    Support through the OS2AVEN forum, to
100033,340 in section 1.

    Internet:

    E-mail address: 100033.340@compuserve.com

Special Information

    Technical support for Galleria primarily is
through the OS2AVEN forum on CompuServe
(users should address queries to ID 100033,340 in
section 1). Limited support is available by E-mail,
fax, or snailmail. No phone support is available.
Support is on a best-effort basis and is free.

Black Ice Software, Inc.

▶ ColorFax for Windows
▶ Faxview for Windows
▶ GIF SDK for Windows
▶ GrabMe Screen Capture Utility
▶ IMAGE SDK for Windows
▶ IMAGE SDK Plus for Windows
▶ PCX & DCX SDK for Windows
▶ TARGA SDK for Windows
▶ TIFF SDK for Windows

Voice, Standard Support: 603-673-1019

Fax Support: 603-672-4112

Online Computer Support

E-mail: Blackice @ MV.MV.COM

CompuServe:
Keyword: GOBLACKICE

☎ Please include as much information as possible and include the serial number.

The Blue Ribbon SoundWorks

Voice, Standard Support: 404-315-0212
Standard support is available, depending upon specific products:
Windows Products: 9 AM to 5:30 PM, Eastern Time, Monday to Friday.
Amiga Products: 1 PM to 5:30 PM, Eastern Time, Monday to Friday.
SGI Indigo Products: 9 AM to 5:30 PM, Eastern Time, Monday to Friday.
Technical support for all Blue Ribbon products is free for a period of 60 consecutive days after purchase.

BMDP Statistical Software, Inc.

Voice, Standard Support: 310-207-8800 (with 24-hour technical support voicemail)
Standard support is available 8 AM to 5 PM, Pacific Time, Monday to Friday.

Fax Support: 310-207-8844

Online Computer Support

E-mail: SUPPORT@BMDP.BMDP.COM

BMDP Statistical Software, Inc.

Boca Research, Inc.

▶ Memory cards and modems

Voice, Standard Support: 407-241-8088
 Standard support is available 8 AM to 6:30 PM,
 Eastern Time, Monday to Friday.

Priority Support: 900-555-4900
 The 900 priority support line is open from 8:00 AM
 to 8:00 PM, Eastern Time, Monday to Friday. The
 cost is $2 per minute.

Fax Support: 407-997-0918

QuickFax: 407-995-9456

Online Computer Support

 Computer Support via Boca Research's BBS:
 407-241-1601

BookMaker Corp.

▶ ClickBook–transforms a Windows document into
 a booklet

Voice, Standard Support: 415-354-8166
 Standard support is available 8 AM to 5 PM, Pacific
 Time, Monday to Friday.

Fax Support: 415-856-4734

Online Computer Support

 Computer support via BookMaker's BBS:
 415-354-8164
 This BBS is for downloads and uploads. There is
 no E-mail on this BBS.

 CompuServe: 72662,3622
 Keyword: GO MAKER

B

Borland

Voice, Standard Support:

Standard support is available 6 AM to 5 PM, Pacific Time, Monday through Friday. Up-and-running support is free to registered users and depends on the individual products:

Borland C++/Turbo C++	408-461-9133
Borland Office	408-461-9199
Borland Pascal/Turbo Pascal	408-461-9177
dBASE (DOS)	408-431-9060
dBASE for Windows	408-461-9110
Paradox (DOS)	408-461-9155
Paradox for Windows	408-461-9166
ReportSmith PC/SQL	408-461-9150

Automated Phone Support: 800-524-8420

900 Advisor Line:

Adviser lines are open 6 AM to 5 PM, Pacific Time, Monday through Friday:

Borland C++/Turbo C++ (DOS)	900-555-1004
Borland C++/Turbo C++ (Windows)	900-555-1002
Borland C++/Turbo C++ (OS/2)	900-555-1005
Borland Pascal/Turbo Pascal	900-555-1007
dBASE (DOS)	900-555-1003
dBASE for Windows	900-555-1009
Paradox (DOS)	900-555-1000
Paradox for Windows	900-555-1006
ReportSmith PC/SQL	900-555-1011

Credit Card Adviser Line:

Adviser lines are open 6 AM to 5 PM, Pacific Time, Monday through Friday:

Borland C++/Turbo C++ (DOS)	800-368-3366
Borland C++/Turbo C++ (Windows)	800-782-5558

Borland C++/Turbo C++ (OS/2)	800-437-8884
Borland Pascal/Turbo Pascal	800-344-2266
dBASE (DOS)	800-368-9222
dBASE for Windows	800-285-1118
Paradox (DOS)	800-468-9990
Paradox for Windows	800-452-1333
ReportSmith PC/SQL	800-673-2288

Incident Line

Call between 8 AM and 5 PM, Pacific Time,
Monday through Friday.

InterBase: 800-550-4888

Client/Server Connectivity: 800-839-9777

Priority Support

Personal Assist, Expert Assist: 800-523-7070
(Open 6 AM to 5 PM, Monday through Friday)
Developer Assist, Help Desk Assist: 800-636-7778
(Open 8 AM to 5 PM, Monday through Friday)

Fax Support: 800-822-4269

Online Computer Support

Computer Support via Borland's BBS: 408-431-5096

CompuServe: Type GO BORLAND

BIX: Type JOIN BORLAND

GEnie: Type BORLAND

Internet: FTP suite: borland.com

Worldwide Support

Australia
Phone: 61-2-911-1000
Fax: 61-2-911-1011

Canada
Phone: 416-229-6000 or 800-461-3327
Fax: 416-229-6123

Europe (except Denmark, Norway)
Phone: 33-1-41-23-11-00
Fax: 33-1-41-23-11-99

Denmark, Norway
Phone: 45-22-62-89-00
Fax: 45-22-62-89-01

Asia
Phone: 852-540-4380
Fax: 852-858-3403

Japan
Phone: 81-3-5350-9370
Fax: 81-3-5350-9390

Latin America
Phone: 408-431-1074
Fax: 408-431-4310

United Kingdom
Phone: 44-734-320-022
Fax: 44-734-320-016

Bright Star

Voice, Standard Support: 206-644-4343
Standard support is available 8:15 AM to 4:45 PM,
Pacific Time, Monday to Friday.

Priority Support: 900-370-5583 (Automated Hint
Line)
This is 75¢ per minute and is available 24 hours,
7 days a week.

Hint Fax: 206-562-4223

Fax Support: 206-644-7697

24-hour Automated Technical Support
206-644-4343
Automated support is available 24 hours, 7 days
a week.

Online Computer Support

Computer Support via Sierra's BBS: 206-644-0112
(23 hours a day)

CompuServe:
Sierra ID: 76004,2143
  GO GAMEAPUB
Dynamix ID: 72662,1174
  GO GAMECPUB
Customer Service ID: 70007,1265
Sierra BBS via CS: GO SIERRA

OnLine Mall: GO SI

America OnLine: Keyword: SIERRA

Worldwide Support

United Kingdom: 44-734-303171
  Fax Support: 44-734-303362
  Standard support is available 9 AM to 5 PM,
  Monday to Friday.

24-hour Automated Technical Support:
Continental Europe (France): 33-1-46-01-4650
Hint Fax: 33-1-46-31-7172
Hint Line: 33-1-36-68-4650
Hint Lines: 44-734-304004 (older games)
            44-891-660660 (new games)
            44-190-336516 (German line)

BBS in United Kingdom: 44-734-304227

Brighton Beach Software

▶ Shareware
▶ JokeBag the ScreenSaver–Windows screen saver
▶ WinType Typing Speed Test System–Windows
  shareware

Voice, Standard Support: 613-822-2848

Fax Support: 613-822-2858

Brother International Corp.

- ▶ Printers and word processors (laptop versions)
- ▶ Fax machines
- ▶ P-Touch systems
- ▶ Filling machines
- ▶ Industrial sewing machines
- ▶ Specialized products

Voice, Standard Support: 800-284-4357
Standard support is available 24 hours, 7 days a week.

Worldwide Support
Quebec (Canada): 514-685-0600

Manchester (Europe): 44-61-3300-6531

Spain: 346-359-7199

Brazil: 55-11-223-2211

☎ A complete listing of international service is available through the standard support number.

Online Computer Support

Computer Support via Brother International's BBS: 714-859-2610
This BBS is accessible by printers.

Support also is available for Brother International Corp. products by calling the main customer service number: 901-373-6256.

ByteSize Software

- ▶ Bible Library (CD-ROM)
- ▶ Bibles & Religion (CD-ROM)
- ▶ Holy Bible (CD-ROM)

- ▶ MAXIMUM Windows Shareware Collection on CD-ROM
- ▶ The New Bible Library (CD-ROM)

Voice, Standard Support: 800-23-BYTES

Fax Support: 813-925-0174

C

Cactus Development Company, Inc.

Voice, Standard Support: 512-453-2244
Standard support is available 2 PM to 9 PM,
Central Time, Monday to Friday, and 10 AM to 2
PM, Central Time, Saturday.

Fax Support: 512-453-3757

Online Computer Support

Computer Support via Cactus League's BBS:
512-453-3155

CompuServe: 72662,1356
Keyword: GO CACTUS

GEnie: R.RHOADES1

Special Information
Cactus Development Company, Inc. is an award-
winning developer of sports simulation software.
For more information, GO CACTUS.

Cadre Technologies, Inc.

- ▶ AC100 Task View–software analysis tool for Ada
- ▶ Atron Evaluator–software testing tool
- ▶ DB Designer
- ▶ ObjectTeam
- ▶ PathMap–CASE reverse engineering package
- ▶ PCSA–CASE tools
- ▶ Software Analysis Workstation (SAW)
- ▶ Teamwork for OS/2
- ▶ Teamwork/PCSA–DOS-based structured analysis tool

Voice, Standard Support: 401-351-5950 or
800-743-2273

Fax Support: 401-455-6800

Worldwide Support
Switzerland
Voice, Standard Support: 41223622251
Fax Support: 41223610785

Calcomp

▶ Digitizers
▶ Drawing Slate
▶ Drawing Board 3
▶ Scanners
▶ Printers via another Calcomp division

Voice, Standard Support: 800-458-5880
Standard support is available 7:30 AM to 4:00 PM, Central Time, Monday to Friday.

Fax Support: 602-948-5508

Online Computer Support
Computer Support via Calcomp's BBS: 714-236-3045

CompuServe: via E-mail

Worldwide Support
Southwest Europe: 011-44-734-320032

Northern Europe: 011-31-20-5457200

Central Europe: 011-49-2131-9550

Calculus, Inc.

▶ Expansion hardware
▶ Advanced EZ-Fax for Networks AVL96
▶ Advanced EZ-Fax for Networks AVS96
▶ EZ-Fax for Networks–hardware/software package
▶ EZ-Fax96 fax board
▶ EZ-Faxit fax/modem board
▶ EZ-FAXit for Windows
▶ IntelliModem 144
▶ Superfax fax board

Voice, Standard Support: 305-481-2334

Fax Support: 305-481-1866

Alternate Voice, Standard Support: 415-390-8770

Alternate Fax Support: 415-390-9588

Caliber

▶ IBM-compatible machine
▶ Microsoft products (Word for Windows, DOS)
▶ Complete hard system

Voice, Standard Support: 408-942-1220
Standard support is available 8:30 AM to 5:30 PM, Pacific Time, Monday to Friday. This support is free with a 1- or 2-year warranty. Free repair/replacement also is included in the warranty.

Fax Support: 408-942-1345
Be sure your fax is to the attention of the technical department.

Cambrix Publishing

▶ CD-ROMs

Voice, Standard Support: 818-992-8484
Standard support is available 8 AM to 6 PM, Pacific Time, Monday to Friday.

Fax Support: 818-992-8781

Campbell Services, Inc.

▶ OnTime Enterprise for NetWare–group scheduling software
▶ OnTime for DOS–personal calendar/to-do list manager Software
▶ OnTime for Networks–group scheduling software
▶ OnTime for Windows–business productivity software

Campbell Services, Inc.

- ▶ OnTime Interactive Voice Response System
- ▶ PhoneBook–personal information manager

Voice, Standard Support: 810-559-5955
Support is free for network products and pay-per-call for single user products.

Fax Support: 810-559-1034

Fax-back: 810-559-5955

Online Computer Support

Computer Support via Campbell's BBS: 810-559-6434

CompuServe: Keyword: GO ONTIME

Internet: E-mail address: support@ontime.com

MCI-Mail:
EMS:ONTIME MBX:SUPPORT
MHS:SUPPORT@ONTIME

Canon Printers

- ▶ Laser/Bubble Jet printers
- ▶ Computers
- ▶ Laptops
- ▶ Subnotebooks
- ▶ Desktops
- ▶ Scanners

Voice, Standard Support: 800-423-2366
Standard support is available 5 AM to 8 PM, Pacific Time, Monday through Friday, and 8 AM to 3 PM, Saturday.

Fax Support via Fax-back: 800-922-9068
You will receive an option list and download on an index. This fax accepts up to four documents in one call.

Online Computer Support

> *Computer Support via Canon's BBS:* 714-438-3325 (14.4K)
>
> *CompuServe:* 800-848-8990
> GO CANAN
> GO CCSI

☎ Canon also offers support through GEnie and America OnLine.

Worldwide Support
Italy
> Canon Printer: 39-2-58010997 168 (Laser/Bubble Jet printers)

Canyon Software

▶ Drag and File–Windows File Manager replacement (shareware)
▶ Drag and View–file viewers for Windows
▶ Drag and View Gold–DWG CAD file viewer for Windows
▶ Drag and View Plus–file viewers for Windows
▶ Drag and Zip–ZIP file viewer and extractor (shareware)
▶ Hard Disk Director (shareware)

Voice, Standard Support: 415-382-7999

Fax Support: 415-382-7998

Online Computer Support

> *CompuServe:* 71320,1277

Carry Associates

Voice, Standard Support: 813-642-9126 (ask for Larry Martin)

Fax Support: 813-642-1007

> *CompuServe:* 72662,3616
> Type: GO CARRY. Support can be obtained via E-mail or, preferably, a public message in Carry's Section in the OS2BVENDOR: Forum, Carry Associates, Section 5. You can find a short description of all of the Carry Associates Products in the ALLSHT.ZIP file in Lib 5 of the OS2BVEN Forum.

Cedar Software

- ▶ Fractal Graphics
- ▶ Fractal Graphics 3D
- ▶ Fractal Graphics Animation Upgrade
- ▶ Fractal Graphics for Windows (book/disk/CD-ROM)
- ▶ FractalVision Screen Animator for Windows
- ▶ FractalVision: Put Fractals to Work for You (book/disk)

Voice, Standard Support: 802-888-5275

Fax Support: 802-888-3009

Central Point Software, Inc.

- ▶ Anti-Virus for DOS–virus-protection software
- ▶ Anti-Virus for Netware–virus-protection software
- ▶ Anti-Virus for Windows–virus-protection software
- ▶ Backup–backup program from PC Tools Deluxe
- ▶ Backup for Windows–backup program
- ▶ Commute–remote computing application
- ▶ Scrapbook+ for Windows–graphics database
- ▶ Copy II PC–backup utility
- ▶ Copy II PC Deluxe option board
- ▶ PC Tools–software utilities package
- ▶ PC Tools for Windows–software utilities package
- ▶ Safe Six–virus protection update for MS-DOS

Voice, Standard Support: 800-278-6657 or 800-847-8766

Alternate Voice, Standard Support: 503-690-8080

Fax Support: 503-690-8083

FaxBack (fax-on-demand): 503-690-2660 or 800-626-2778

Online Computer Support

Computer Support via Central Point's BBS: 503-690-6650

Worldwide Support

Canada
Voice, Standard Support: 905-890-5851 or 800-278-6657
Fax Support: 905-890-5381

Germany
Voice, Standard Support: 49896700710
Fax Support: 498967007120

Australia
Voice, Standard Support: 6124109801
Fax Support: 6124109987

France
Voice, Standard Support: 33141191919
Fax Support: 33141191920

England
Voice, Standard Support: 081-848-1414
Fax Support: 081-569-1017

Centron Software Inc.

▶ Advanced Casino Strategy–video poker and blackjack games
▶ Baccarat Master
▶ Blackjack Ace

Centron Software Inc.

- ► Casino Master
- ► Casino Master Gold Edition–includes seven games
- ► Casino Master Windows
- ► Craps Master
- ► Crossword Creator
- ► Games Master–assorted game collection for Windows
- ► Poker Master
- ► Puzzle Master–crossword puzzles
- ► Roulette Master
- ► Wordsearch Creator–puzzle-making program for Windows

Voice, Standard Support: 910-692-2009 or 800-848-2424

Fax Support: 910-692-2173

CH Products

Voice, Standard Support: 619-598-2518
Standard support is available 8 AM to 4:15 PM, Pacific Time, Monday to Friday.

Fax Support: 619-598-2524

Online Computer Support

Computer Support via CH Products' BBS: 619-598-3224

CI$: This Address or GO GAMEDPUB

Delphi: CHProducts

GEnie: CH.Products

America OnLine: CHProducts

Internet: E-mail address: CHProducts@aol.com

Changeling Software, Inc.

Voice, Standard Support: 203-292-5087

Fax Support: 203-292-5089

Online Computer Support

CompuServe:

Mac Entertainment Forum:

Game Publishers C Forum: Type: GO CHANGELING

America OnLine: Address: Changeling Keyword: CHANGELING

Mac Game Forum: Keyword: MACFUN

E-World: Mac Game Forum Keyword: CHANGELING

AppleLink: Address: Changeling

Internet: E-mail address: Changeling@aol.com
comp.sys.mac.games (discussion/support)
cu.mich archives (files)
sumex.aim archives (files)

Cheyenne Communications, Inc.

► NetWare tape backups
► Bitfax/Bitcom for DOS
► Bitfax/Bitcom for Windows
► Bitfax Professional

Voice, Standard Support: 510-490-9470
Standard support is available 8 AM to 5 PM, Pacific Time, Monday to Friday.

Fax Support via fax-back: 516-629-4675

Online Computer Support

Computer Support via Cheyenne's BBS: 510-490-6637

CompuServe: 72662,2254

Cheyenne Software Inc.

Voice, Standard Support: 800-CHEY-TEC (243-9832)
Standard support is available 8 AM to 6:30 PM,
Eastern Time, Monday to Friday to speak to a
representative directly. Otherwise, 6:30 PM to
10:00 PM, Eastern Time, Monday to Friday, and
10 AM to 4 PM, Eastern Time, on Saturday and
Sunday, Cheyenne works on a callback basis.

Fax Support: 516-484-3493

FaxBack: 516-629-4675
(InfoFax Service) Technical information including
technical tips, data sheets, and certified device lists
can be obtained through our FaxBack service.
From outside the United States, you must call from
a fax phone to obtain these documents.

Online Computer Support

Computer Support via Cheyenne's BBS: 516-484-3445
You can use any ASCII terminal emulation
program. This BBS handles up to 14.4K with
8 data bits, no parity, and 1 stop bit. This BBS
also can be used to upload information to our
technical support representatives.

CompuServe: Type: GO CHEYENNE

Internet:
ftp cheyenne.chey.com
ftp.chey.com
ftp 199.29.133.2
The user is called ftp; the password is your
Internet identification (i.e. joez@chey.com).

Special Information

If you are calling outside the United States, you
can reach Cheyenne at 516-484-5110. There are
no additional charges. Messages can be left on
their voice system at any time.

Cheyenne Software Inc.

C

Worldwide Support
France: 011-33-1-39231880 or 011-33-1-39633341

Choice Computing
▶ Truecad For Windows–full-featured CAD package

Voice, Standard Support: 415-428-0131 or
   800-828-2770

Fax Support: 415-949-2615

Chronologic Corp.
▶ Instant Recall–personal information management
▶ Instant Recall for Windows–personal information
   management

Voice, Standard Support: 602-293-3100 or
   800-848-4970

Fax Support: 602-293-0709

Cirque Corp.
▶ Glyde Point

Voice, Standard Support: 800-454-3375
   Standard support is available 8 AM to 4 PM,
   Central Time, Monday to Friday.

   Fax Support: 801-467-0208

Citrix Systems, Inc.
▶ Multiuser Link–terminal-emulation software
▶ Multiuser version of OS/2 operating system
▶ Wincredible–Windows application server on a
   LAN
▶ Winview for Networks–application server with
   remote access

Voice, Standard Support: 305-755-0559 or
   800-437-7503

Citrix Systems, Inc.

Fax Support: 305-341-6880

Online Computer Support

Computer Support via Citrix Systems' BBS Phone: 305-346-9004

Classic Software, Inc.

▶ Btrv++–C++ class library for Novell Btrieve
▶ Btrvgen++–class/code generator and data dictionary for Btrv++
▶ Cbtrv–C library for Btrieve
▶ DDF Maker–Windows-hosted Btrieve DDF file editor
▶ Vbtrv Control Pack–VBX custom controls for Btrieve programming
▶ Vbtrv for DOS–function call interface to Novell Btrieve
▶ Vbtrv for Windows–Btrieve interface VBX
▶ Vbtrv/C++–Btrieve interface toolkit

Voice, Standard Support: 313-677-0732 or 800-677-2952

Fax Support: 313-971-3287

Clear Software, Inc.

▶ Allclear–flowcharting software
▶ Allclear for Windows–flowcharting software
▶ CLEAR Org Chart for Windows–organizational charts
▶ Clear+ for C–automatic C program documentation
▶ Clear+ For Dbase–automatic dBASE program documentation
▶ Programmer's Power Pack–Clear+ for dBASE and C combined
▶ Trackit–point-and-shoot environment to build libraries

C

Voice, Standard Support: 617-965-6755 or
800-338-1759

Fax Support: 617-965-5310

Online Computer Support

Computer Support via Clear Software's BBS:
617-965-5406

CoActive

▶ Coactive Connectors for PCs and Macs

Voice, Standard Support: 415-802-2882
Standard support is available 8:30 AM to 3:30 PM,
Pacific Time, Monday to Friday.

Fax Support: 415-802-1088

Online Computer Support

Computer Support via CoActive's BBS: 415-802-1077

CompuServe: 71031,2761

Cogent Data Technologies, Inc.

Voice, Standard Support: 206-378-2929
Standard support is available 8 AM to 5 PM, Pacific
Time, Monday to Friday.

Fax Support: 206-378-2882

Online Computer Support

Computer Support via Cogent's BBS: 206-378-5405

CompuServe: !GO COGENT

Internet: support@cogentdata.com

CogniTech

Voice, Standard Support: 404-518-3285
First 30 days after the first call are free of charge.
After that, $20 per call or $59.95 for a year's worth

of unlimited support calls and use of an 800 number. Fax, automated faxback service, E-mail, and Forum responses are free. Patches are posted regularly on CompuServe and Cognitech's BBS for the latest problem solutions that are available.

Fax Support: 404-518-9137

Faxback: 404-640-3012

Online Computer Support

> *Computer Support via Cognitech's BBS:* 404-518-7617

> *CompuServe:* 72662,3417
> Type: GO SHARKWARE (CogniTech Corp.)

Cognitronix

▶ Code Manager–Windows text search utility
▶ Searcher–Windows search utility
▶ Searcher Professional–Windows text search utility

Voice, Standard Support: 619-549-8955 or 800-217-0932

Coktel

Voice, Standard Support: 206-644-4343
> Standard support is available 8:15 AM to 4:45 PM, Pacific Time, Monday to Friday.

Priority Support: 900-370-5583
> (Automated Hint Line) This is $0.75 per minute and is available 24 hours, 7 days a week.

Hint Fax: 206-562-4223

Fax Support: 206-644-7697

24-hour Automated Technical Support: 206-644-4343
> Automated support is available 24 hours, 7 days a week.

C

Online Computer Support

Computer Support via Sierra's BBS: 206-644-0112
(23 hours a day)

CompuServe:
Sierra ID: 76004,2143
  GO GAMEAPUB
Dynamix ID: 72662,1174
  GO GAMECPUB
Customer Service ID: 70007,1265
Sierra BBS via CS: GO SIERRA
OnLine Mall: GO SI

America OnLine: Keyword: SIERRA

Worldwide Support
United Kingdom: 44-734-303171
  Fax Support: 44-734-303362
  Standard support is available 9 AM to 5 PM,
  Monday to Friday.

24-hour Automated Technical Support:
Continental Europe (France): 33-1-46-01-4650
Hint Fax: 33-1-46-31-7172
Hint Line: 33-1-36-68-4650
Hint Lines: 44-734-304004 (older games)
             44-891-660660 (new games)
             44-190-336516 (German line)

BBS in United Kingdom: 44-734-304227

Colorado Memory Systems

▶ Colorado Backup for DOS–hard disk backup
   software
▶ Colorado Backup for Windows–hard disk backup
   software
▶ DJ-10 40MB tape drive, expandable to 120MB
▶ DJ-20 80MB tape drive, expandable to 250MB
▶ Jumbo 120MB and 250MB cartridge tape drives

Colorado Memory Systems

- ▶ Jumbo Trakker tape backup drive using a PC parallel port
- ▶ Powerdat tape backup system, internal or external
- ▶ Powertape QIC tape backup system, internal or external
- ▶ QFA-500 150MB tape backup unit
- ▶ QFA-700 500MB tape backup unit
- ▶ Turbo-Compression–cartridge tape drive controller boards

Voice, Standard Support: 303-669-8000 or 800-346-9881

Fax Support: 303-667-0921

Online Computer Support

> *Computer Support via Colorado Memory System's BBS Phone: 303-679-0650*

The Complete PCS, Inc.

- ▶ Modems, faxes, scanners

Voice, Standard Support: 407-997-8062
Standard support is available 8 AM to 6:30 PM, Eastern Time, Monday to Friday.

Priority support: 900-555-4900
The 900 priority support line is open from 8 AM to 8 PM, Eastern Time, Monday to Friday. The cost is $2 per minute.

Fax Support: 407-997-0918

QuickFax: 407-997-9645

Online Computer Support

> *Computer Support via Complete PCS's BBS: 407-997-9130*

C

CompuServe Information Service

- ► CompuServe–online telecommunications network
- ► CompuServe Information Manager for Windows (Wincim)
- ► CompuServe Navigator (Csnav)–Windows interface software for CIS
- ► CompuServecd–monthly electronic magazine on CD-ROM

Voice, Standard Support: 614-457-8600 or 800-621-1253

Fax Support: 614-457-0348

Online Computer Support

Internet: Email: Sales@CIS.CompuServe.com

Computer Associates International, Inc.

- ► CA-Unicenter
- ► CA-Unicenter/Star
- ► CA-Openingres
- ► CA-OpenROAD
- ► CA-Visual Realia
- ► CA-Visual Objects
- ► CA-ACCPAC
- ► CA-Visual Express
- ► CA-PRMS
- ► CA-Masterpiece
- ► CA-HRISMA
- ► CA-TOP SECRET
- ► CA-ACF2
- ► CA-ASM2
- ► CA-SCHEDULER
- ► CA-IDMS
- ► CA-DATACOM
- ► CA-CAS
- ► CA-Warehouse BOSS

Computer Associates International, Inc.

Voice, Standard Support:

There are specific phone numbers for each and every product. The following are general numbers for each North American Support Center:

Islandia (Long Island) Support Center:	516-342-5224
Alameda Support Center:	510-769-1400
Andover Support Center:	508-691-4200
Birmingham Support Center:	205-324-2682
Culver City Support Center:	310-216-0818
Fort Lee Support Center:	201-592-0009
Irving Support Center:	214-556-7100
Lisle Support Center:	708-505-6600
Marietta Support Center:	404-953-9276
Midvale Support Center:	801-561-8914
Mount Laurel Support Center:	609-273-9100
Princeton Support Center:	908-874-9100
Reston Support Center:	703-709-4500
San Diego Support Center:	619-452-4454
Santa Clara Support Center:	408-562-8800
Santa Rosa Support Center:	707-528-6560
Vancouver Support Center:	604-733-2343
Westwood Support Center:	617-326-8251

Standard support is available 9 AM to 7 PM, Eastern Time, Monday through Friday. Support is free for the first 90 days and is available thereafter on either an annual fee basis or on a pay-by-use basis.

Fax Support:

Simply Accounting:	516-342-5067
Simply Money/Simply Tax:	516-342-5194
CA-BPI Accounting:	516-342-5192
ACCPAC Plus Accounting:	516-342-5190

Computer Associates International, Inc.

Online Computer Support

Computer Support via Computer Associates' BBS:
516-434-1753

This bulletin board provides support for the following products: ACCPAC Plus Accounting, CA-BPI Accounting, CA-Clipper, CA-Easytrieve, CA-IDMS/PC, CA-IDMS Unix, CA-Pan/LCM, CA-Panaudit, CA-Panvalet, CA-PRMS, CA-Realia, CA-SuperCalc, CA- SuperProject, CA-Telon, and Simple Money

CompuServe:
Type: GO CLIPPER (for CA-Clipper Forum)
Type: GO CAIDEV (for CA Development Tools forum)
Type: GO CAIPRO (for CA Productivity Tools forum)
Type: GO SIMPLY (for 4Home Productions Simply forum)

Worldwide Support

Australia: 61-2-923-2066

Brazil: 55-11-536-4366

Canada: 905-676-6700

France: 33-1-40-97-50-50

Germany: 49-6151-949-0

Holland: 31-3402-483-45

Italy: 39-2-90-464-1

Spain: 34-3-22781-00

Switzerland: 41-1-814-03-00

U.K.: 44-753-5777-33

Special Information

For nonretail products, Computer Associates provides CA-TCC: Total Client Care, which is a

Computer Associates International, Inc.

major extension to existing support programs. CA-TCC provides access to the Computer Associates centralized client support database via CompuServe or Advantis, the IBM Information Network (IIN). For more information on CA-TCC, contact the CA-TCC hotline at 800-338-6720.

Also for nonretail products, Computer Associates provides 24-hour technical support, 365 days a year. There are two kinds of services available: primary and secondary. Primary service is provided during normal business hours (9 AM to 7 PM, Eastern Time, Monday through Friday). Emergency service is available after primary service hours, for severity 1 problems only.

CompuView Products, Inc.

- ▶ Edit Plus–word processor
- ▶ Vedit–text editor with split-screen windows
- ▶ Vedit Jr–entry-level text editor
- ▶ Vedit Plus (VEDIT+)–text editor with macro programming
- ▶ Vspell

Voice, Standard Support: 313-996-1299 or 800-45-VEDIT

Fax Support: 313-996-1308

Connectsoft

- ▶ E-Mail Connection–Windows E-mail automation software

Voice, Standard Support: 206-881-8251 or 800-234-9497

Fax Support: 06-869-0252

Corel System

► Corel Draw
► Corel Gallery
► Corel Flow
► Ventura

Voice, Standard Support

PHOTO CD, SCSI Support: 613-728-1010
This support is available 8 AM to 5 PM, Eastern
Time, Monday to Friday.

DRAW, VENTURA, GALLERY, FLOW: 800-818-1848
This support is available 4 AM-8 PM, Eastern Time,
Monday to Friday.

Voice, Priority Support: 800-818-1848
900-896-8800 (This number is pay-for-service at
$2 per minute.)

Fax Support: 613-761-9176
Fax in a detailed description of your problem,
and the technical department will get back to
you within 72 hours.

Online Computer Support

Computer Support via Corel's BBS: 613-728-4752 or
613-761-7798

CompuServe: Type: GO COREL

☎ Support also is offered on UNIX versions of
DRAW: 613-728-8200, ext. 1867

CoStar

► Address writer/labeler
► Printers
► Address writers
► Labels
► Software

CoStar

Voice, Standard Support: 203-661-9700, option 4
  Standard support is available 9 AM to 5 PM,
  Eastern Time, Monday to Friday.

Fax Support: 203-661-1540
  Fax in a detailed description of your problem. Be
  sure to include your name, company, and any
  special instructions that are needed.

Online Computer Support

  Computer Support via CoStar's BBS: 203-661-6292

  America OnLine: Keyword: GO COSTAR

  CompuServe: 75300,2225
  Type: GO COSTAR

  AppleLink: COSTAR

  E-world: COSTAR

Creative Assistance Software

▶ NetPM–LAN server management and performance
  monitor
▶ WatchLogon–password error monitor for LAN
  Server 3.0/4.0

Voice, Standard Support: 704-544-0001

Creative Labs, Inc.

Voice, Standard Support: 405-742-6622
  Standard support is available 8 AM to 10 PM,
  Central Time, Monday through Sunday, except
  for holidays. When you call or fax, Creative Labs
  asks that you have the following information:
  Base 1/0 addess used by your card.
  Error message on the screen and how it came
  about.
  Information on the adapter card that conflicts
  with your card.

Fax Support: 405-742-6633

Online Computer Support

> *Computer Support via Creative Labs' BBS:*
> 405-742-6660

Worldwide Support

Singapore:

> Phone: 405-742-6622
> Fax: 65-773-0353
> BBS: 65-776-2423
> Standard support is available 9 AM to 6 PM,
> Singapore Time, Monday to Friday, and 9 AM to
> 1 PM, Saturday.

Crescent Software, Inc.

- ▶ Dialogic–generate text-based dialog boxes for QuickBASIC
- ▶ Don Malin's Cross Reference Utility (XREF)–for BASIC
- ▶ Graphics Workshop–BASIC graphics routine toolkit
- ▶ Graphpak–BASIC subroutine library for graphics functions
- ▶ Graphpak Professional
- ▶ Laserpak–BASIC library
- ▶ Netpak Professional–DLL access to network services
- ▶ P.D.Q.–replacement library for QuickBASIC BCOM
- ▶ Pdqcomm for Windows–libraries and programming utilities
- ▶ Qbase–BASIC subroutine library for screen design
- ▶ Qbase Report
- ▶ Quickmenu–DOS shell
- ▶ Quickpak
- ▶ Quickpak Professional–BASIC library

- ▶ Quickpak Professional for Windows–Visual BASIC library
- ▶ Quickpak Scientific–BASIC library
- ▶ Quickscreen–screen generator
- ▶ Xref for Visual BASIC–cross reference developer's tool

Voice, Standard Support: 203-438-5300 or 800-352-2742

Fax Support: 203-431-4626

Online Computer Support

CompuServe: 70662,2605

Crosswise Corp.

- ▶ Face to Face Version 2.0 for both Windows and Macintosh

Voice, Standard Support: 408-459-9060
Standard support is available 8:30 AM to 5:00 PM, Pacific Time, Monday to Friday.

Fax Support: 408-426-3859

Online Computer Support
You can obtain a variety of company and product information on the Crosswise Mosaic server at "www.crosswise.com" and the Crosswise Gopher server at "gopher.crosswise.com."

AppleLink: E-mail address: CROSSWISE

CompuServe: Type: GO CROSSWISE

Internet: E-mail address: support@crosswise.com

Special Information
Crosswise offers several technical support options:

First Meeting Service: If you would like Crosswise's help getting started with Face to Face, call

C

408-459-9054 and have your first meeting with Crosswise Customer Support. They will take you through a quick demo of Face to Face and show you how to share documents in real time over the Internet, a modem, or ISDN. If you have not yet licensed a copy of Face to Face, you can download the Face to Face Listener and use it to have a first meeting with them.

Telephone Support: You can talk to a Crosswise support technician by calling 408-459-9054 any time between 8:30 AM and 5:00 PM, Pacific Time, Monday to Friday.

Ctrlalt Associates

▶ Stackey and Batutil Version 4.1

Online Computer Support

CompuServe: Type: GO PCSVEN

Internet: 76004.1664@CompuServe.com on Internet

CyberCorp, Inc.

▶ Cyberdesk

Voice, Standard Support: 404-424-6240

Fax Support: 404-424-8995

Online Computer Support

CompuServe: 72662,1267
WinapE forum; section 10

Internet: E-mail address: cyber@netcom.com

Cyco International

- ▶ Autobase–graphical database for AutoCAD drawings
- ▶ Automanager–AutoCAD drawing management utility
- ▶ Automanager Classic–AutoCAD drawing management tool
- ▶ Automanager Classic For Windows–AutoCAD drawing management tool
- ▶ Automanager Classic/ADS–AutoCAD drawing management tool
- ▶ Automanager Organizer–AutoCAD drawing management
- ▶ Automanager Professional–AutoCAD drawing management utility
- ▶ Automanager Workflow–manage AutoCAD drawings (was Autobase)
- ▶ Automanager Workflow For Windows–AutoCAD drawing management
- ▶ Autosave
- ▶ Flying Dutchman, The–file-transfer software

Voice, Standard Support: 404-634-3302 or 800-323-2926

Fax Support: 404-633-4604

Online Computer Support

Computer Support via Cyco International's BBS Phone: 404-634-1441

CompuServe: 75170,675

Worldwide Support
Netherlands
Alternate Voice, Standard Support: 703993054
Alternate Fax Support: 703191344

D

Data Access Corp.

▶ Dataflex

Voice, Standard Support: 305-232-3142
  Support for WinQl/FlexQL: 305-238-4772
  Standard support is available 9 AM to 5:30 PM,
  Eastern Time, Monday to Friday. Data Access
  offers 90 days of free support on all products.
  Following the 90 days, a one-year support
  contract must be purchased for continuing phone
  support. The one-year support contract is for
  unlimited calls on a toll line. The contracts range
  from $75 to $150 depending on the product.

Online Computer Support

  CompuServe: Type: GO DACCESS
  This forum is always available, even for
  customers without support contracts.

Data Assist, Inc.

▶ MOSAIX–shareware electronic jigsaw puzzle
▶ MOSAIX for Windows–shareware electronic
  jigsaw puzzle
▶ PC-Piano Teacher–shareware music teaching
  program
▶ PC-Quizzer–shareware courseware authoring
  system
▶ Wavepool–sound file creation programming
  language

Voice, Standard Support: 614-888-8088

Fax Support: 614-888-8072

Online Computer Support

  Computer Support via Data Assist's BBS Phone:
  614-888-8056

  Internet: E-mail: brian@aiinet.com

DataEase International

Voice, Standard Support: 203-374-2825
Standard support is available 9 AM to 6 PM,
Eastern Time, Monday through Friday. DataEase
offers 10 free contacts to the Technical Support
Department for all DataEase users from the date
of software registration. Beyond the initial 10
contacts, you can purchase priority support.

Priority Support:
DataEase Personal Support Service ($99) provides
technical support to one specified caller for one
year with a maximum contact allocation.

DataEase Business Support Service ($695)
provides toll-free technical support to five
specified callers for one year with a maximum
contact allocation. Business Support Service
customers receive new product release preview
information, product fix and outstanding
problem lists, and software updates including
DataEase's new software patch technology.

Advanced Technical Support (ATS) provides toll-
free number access to DataEase's most senior
technicians. DataEase recommends ATS for
mission critical applications in the native and
server environments. Basic ATS service is $2,000
annually. Client server support requires an
additional charge. Please call for additional
information.

Pay-By-The-Call: 203-374-2825
Each call is $25 and is billable to your
MasterCard, Visa, or American Express.

Datastorm Technologies, Inc.

- ▶ Hot Wire–file-transfer and disk-management utility
- ▶ Procomm–communications package
- ▶ Procomm for Windows–communications package
- ▶ Procomm Plus–communications package
- ▶ Procomm Plus for Windows–communications package
- ▶ Procomm Plus Network Version–communications package

Voice, Standard Support: 314-875-0530

Online Computer Support

Computer Support via Datastorm Technologies' BBS Phone: 314-875-0503

Deadly Games

- ▶ U-Boat
- ▶ M4
- ▶ Battle Of Britain II
- ▶ Bomber2

Voice, Standard Support: 516-628-1008

Fax Support: 516-628-1039

Online Computer Support

CompuServe: 74431,2470
Type: GO DEADLY

E-World: Deadly Game

America OnLine: Keyword: Deadly G

Dell Computer

- ▶ Notebook PCs: Latitude
- ▶ Desktop and minitower PCs: Dell Dimension, OptiPlex

Dell Computer

- ▶ High-end PC workstations: OmniPlex
- ▶ File servers: PowerEdge

Voice, Standard Support: 800-624-9896 or
512-728-4093
Standard support is available 24 hours a day,
7 days a week.

Priority Support
Priority support is available to major account
customers and government customers.

Fax Support: 800-950-1329
This fax support is automated.

Online Computer Support

Computer Support via Dell's BBS: 512-728-8528

CompuServe: Type: GO DELL

Internet: Via CompuServe

Worldwide Support
Northern Europe
Bray, Ireland
Phone: 353-1-286-0500

Southern Europe
Montpellier, France
Phone: 33-6706-6000

Japan
Tokyo, Japan
Phone: 81-3-5420-7386

Australia
Frenchs Forest, NSW
Phone: 61-2-930-3355

Delrina Corp.

- ▶ Barcode Composer
- ▶ Berkeley Breathed's Opus 'N Bill Brain Saver

- ▶ Delrina Communications Suite–WinFax Pro and WinComm Pro package
- ▶ Dosfax Pro–fax software for DOS
- ▶ Flintstones Screen Saver Collection, The
- ▶ Formflow–forms-based work-flow solution
- ▶ Opus 'N Bill On The Road Again!–screen saver
- ▶ Perform Designer And Filler–forms-generation and filling software
- ▶ Perform Filler & Filler LAN Pack
- ▶ Perform Pro Designer And Filler–forms-generation and filling
- ▶ Perform Pro Filler–forms-filling software
- ▶ Perform Pro Plus–Precanned business forms
- ▶ Perform Video–demo/tutorial video tape
- ▶ Scott Adams Dilbert Screen Saver Collection
- ▶ WinComm Pro–general-purpose communications software for Windows
- ▶ WinFax–fax communication application/driver for Windows
- ▶ WinFax Pro–fax software for Windows
- ▶ WinFax Pro for Networks

Voice, Standard Support: 416-441-3676 or
    800-268-6082
    Alternate Voice Support: 408-363-2345

Fax Support: 416-441-0774
    Alternate Fax Support: 408-363-2340

Support for specific products:

   Alternate Voice, Standard Support: 416-441-1026

   WinFax Pro for Networks Tech Support:
   Voice, Standard Support: 416-441-1928

   Forms products Tech Support:
   Voice, Standard Support: 416-441-3086

Delrina Corp.

WinFax Pro Tech Support:
Voice, Standard Support: 416-443-4396

WinComm Tech Support:
Voice, Standard Support: 416-441-0921

Online Computer Support

Computer Support via Delrina's BBS Phone:
416-441-2752

CompuServe: Type GO DELRINA

DeltaPoint

▶ DeltaGraph Professional for Mac and Windows
▶ FreezeFrame 1 and 2 for Windows
▶ Graphics Tools! for Windows
▶ Animated Desktop for Windows

Voice, Standard Support: 408-375-4700
Standard support is available 7 AM to 5 PM, Pacific Time, Monday to Friday.

Online Computer Support

America OnLine: Keyword: DELTAPOINT

AppleLink: D0067

CompuServe: 76004,1522

Mac Forum: GO MACAVEN

Win Forum: GO WINAPD

Deneba Software

▶ Canvas Drawing
▶ Deneba Artworks
▶ Spelling Coach Professional

Voice, Standard Support: 305-596-5644
Standard support is available 9 AM to 6 PM, Eastern Time, Monday through Friday.

Fax Support: 305-273-9069

Online Computer Support

America OnLine: Forum is DENEBA

CompuServe: 76004,2154
Keyword GO MACACBVEN
Section 15

E-World: DENEBA 1

DeScribe, Inc.

▶ Describe–word processor
▶ DeScribe for OS/2–a native 32-bit word processor for OS/2 2.*x*
▶ DeScribe for NT–a native 32-bit word processor for WindowsNT
▶ DeScribe for Windows–a 16-bit word processor for Windows
▶ DeLights–a CPU monitoring tool for OS/2

Voice, Standard Support: 813-775-1571 or 916-646-1111
Telephone support is free to users with Subscription Edition service at these telephone numbers. Users who are not on Subscription Edition service pay $25.00 per call after the initial two support calls.

Fax Support: 916-923-3447

Online Computer Support

Computer Support via DeScribe's BBS: 916-929-3237

CompuServe: 71333,154
Type: GO DESCRIBE

Prodigy: OS/2 area

Desktop Solutions

▶ From Scratch–shareware recipe program for Windows
▶ JJ Flash–fast shareware Windows launcher

Voice, Standard Support: 516-944-3254

Online Computer Support

Computer Support via Desktop Solution's BBS Phone: 516-536-1091

America OnLine: Keyword: FRANKIMBUR

CompuServe: 74676,3314

Prodigy: KDTR60A

DoMark Software, Inc.

Voice, Standard Support: 415-513-8933 or 415-513-8929

Fax Support: 415-571-0437

Online Computer Support

Computer Support via DoMark's BBS: 415-571-9364

Dragon Systems, Inc.

▶ Dragon VoiceTools–voice-aware application development toolkit
▶ DragonDictate for DOS: Classic Edition–voice recognition w/DSP Power Edition–voice recognition w/DSP Starter Edition–voice recognition w/DSP
▶ DragonDictate for Windows: Classic Edition–voice recognition software Power Edition–voice recognition software Starter Edition–voice recognition software
▶ DragonTalk>To–voice command and control for Windows
▶ DragonWriter

D

- ▶ IBM VoiceType 2–speech-recognition command and control software

Voice, Standard Support: 617-965-5200 or 800-825-5897

Fax Support: 617-527-0372

Dynacomp, Inc.

- ▶ Astroquest-astrology software
- ▶ Backgammon 2.0
- ▶ Bar Code Printer (BCP)
- ▶ Barney O'Blarney's Magic Spells-spelling/math game
- ▶ Bible On Disk, The-King James Version
- ▶ Bowling League Record System II (BLRS II)
- ▶ Bowling League Record System II Expanded Version
- ▶ Bowling League Secretary (shareware)
- ▶ Bridgemaster
- ▶ Bridgemaster II
- ▶ Chess Master 2001
- ▶ Children's Carrousel-early childhood educational software
- ▶ Computer Chef-kitchen database
- ▶ Easy Access-communications program
- ▶ Executive Phone/Mailer-address/phone database/ mailing list
- ▶ Fortune Telling II: Tarot And Geomancy
- ▶ Home Doctor
- ▶ Hometown Demographics
- ▶ On Time! Business Calendar-appointment calendar system
- ▶ PC Planetarium-astronomy software
- ▶ Private Pilot Written Test Simulator
- ▶ Real Estate Resident Expert-real estate analysis

Voice, Standard Support: 716-265-4040

Dynacomp, Inc.

Dynalink Technologies

▶ Clip'nSave 2.0 for Windows–screen capture utility

Main Phone: 514-489-3007

Fax Phone: 514-489-3007

Dynamix

Voice, Standard Support: 206-644-4343
Standard support is available 8:15 AM to 4:45 PM,
Pacific Time, Monday to Friday.

Priority Support: 900-370-5583 (Automated Hint
Line)
This is 75¢ per minute and is available 24 hours,
7 days a week.

Hint Fax: 206-562-4223

Fax Support: 206-644-7697

24-hour Automated Technical Support:
206-644-4343
Automated support is available 24 hours, 7 days
a week.

Online Computer Support

Computer Support via Sierra's BBS: 206-644-0112
(23 hours a day)

CompuServe:
Sierra ID: 76004,2143
  GO GAMEAPUB
Dynamix ID: 72662,1174
  GO GAMECPUB
Customer Service ID: 70007,1265
Sierra BBS via CS: GO SIERRA
OnLine Mall: GO SI

America OnLine: Keyword: SIERRA

D

Worldwide Support
United Kingdom: 44-734-303171
    Fax Support: 44-734-303362
    Standard support is available 9 AM to 5 PM,
    Monday to Friday.

    24-hour Automated Technical Support:
    Continental Europe (France): 33-1-46-01-4650
    Hint Fax: 33-1-46-31-7172
    Hint Line: 33-1-36-68-4650
    Hint Lines: 44-734-304004 (older games)
               44-891-660660 (new games)
               44-190-336516 (German line)

    BBS in United Kingdom: 44-734-304227

Dynamix

Eccentric Software

▶ A Zillion Kajillion Rhymes–Windows rhyming dictionary

Voice, Standard Support: 206-628-2687 or 800-436-6758

Fax Support: 206-628-2681

Eclipse Software, Inc.

▶ Architectural Power Tools–for AutoCAD release 11 for Windows
▶ Facade–face-based 3D building modeler for AutoCAD

Voice, Standard Support: 206-676-6175

Fax Support: 206-676-0921

Edmark Corp.

▶ Bailey's Book House–literacy program for prereaders
▶ Kiddesk–safeguards programs and data from children
▶ Kiddesk Family Edition for Windows
▶ Millie's Math House–basic counting and matching skills
▶ Thinkin' Things–creativity and analytical skills
▶ Touchwindow–portable touch screen

Voice, Standard Support: 206-556-8400 or 800-426-0856

Fax Support: 206-861-8998

Eidolon

▶ Millennium Auction–a single- or multiple-player game for multimedia-equipped Windows PCS's.

E

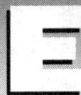

Voice, Standard Support: 718-884-1981
Standard support is available 9 AM to 5 PM,
Eastern Time, Monday to Friday. Before and after
those hours, there's a voice-mail system.

Online Computer Support

CompuServe: 74774,673
Type: GO GAMDPUB (in the Eidolon forum)

Electronic Arts

Voice, Standard Support: 415-572-ARTS
Standard support is available 8:30 AM to 4:30 PM,
Pacific Time, Monday to Friday.

Online Computer Support

CompuServe on three forums:
EASY, GAMEPUB, and VIDPUB

Worldwide Support

United Kingdom: 753-546465

Australia: 075-711-811

New Zealand: +61-75-711-811
Support is available 9 AM to 5 PM, Eastern
Standard Time.

EA Hints & Information Hotline

900-288-HINT (4468)
Call this number for recorded hints, tips, and
passwords. The line is available 24 hours a day,
7 days a week. It is pay-per-use at 75¢ per
minute (95¢ for the first minute).

In Canada, dial 900-451-4873. The rate is $1.15
(Canadian) per minute.

The hotline requires a touch-tone telephone. The
call length is determined by the user; the
average call length is four minutes. Messages are
subject to change without notice.

Electronic Arts

Note to hotline callers: To help you quickly locate the information that you need, Electronic Arts will gladly send you printed menus.

Elo TouchSystems

▶ AccuTouch–resistive touchscreen
▶ IntelliTouch–surface-wave touchscreen

Voice, Standard Support: 615-220-4299

Fax Support: 615-482-6617

Online Computer Support

Computer Support via ELO's BBS: 615-482-9840

CompuServe: GO ELOTOUCH

ELSA

▶ Graphic cards
▶ Monitors
▶ Modems
▶ ISDN adapters

Voice, Standard Support: 49-0-241-9177-211 (computer grafic) 49-0-241-9177-112 (data communication)
Standard support is available 9 AM to 4:30 PM, Monday to Thursday, and 9 AM to 12 PM, Friday.

Fax Support: 49-0-241-9177-600

Online Computer Support

Computer Support via ELSA's BBS:
per modem (up to 28.8Kbit/s): 49-0-241-9177-981
per ISDN: 49-0-241-9177-7800

CompuServe: GO ELSA

E

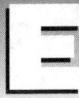

E-MU Systems, Inc.

Voice, Standard Support: 408-438-1921

Online Computer Support

   CompuServe: MIDI A Forum under E-MU Systems

   Internet: Service@@qmmac.emu.com

Enable Software, Inc.

► Enable Business Software
► Enable 4.0 and 4.5–fully Integrated office productivity, including spreadsheet, graphics, word processing, database, and communications modules

Voice, Standard Support: 518-877-8236

Fax Support: 518-877-6354

Online Computer Support

   Computer Support via Enable Software's BBS Phone: 518-877-6316

Epson America

► Ink jet printers: Stylus Color, Stylus 800+, Stylus 1000
► Laser printers: ActionLaser 1400, ActionLaser 1600
► Dot matrix printers: LQ 300, DFX 5000+
► Desktop computers: Action Tower 2000, Action Tower 3000
► Notebook computers: ActionNote 500 series, ActionNote 600 series, ActionNote 700 series

Voice, Standard Support: 800-922-8911 or 800-289-3776

   Standard support is available 6 AM to 6 PM, Pacific Time, Monday through Friday.

Fax Support: 310-782-5284

Online Computer Support

   Computer Support via Epson's BBS: 310-782-4531

   CompuServe: Via BBS forum

Worldwide Support

Canada

   Ontario: 416-498-9955 or 905-478-8866

Latin America

Miami:	305-265-0092
Argentina:	541-322-6898
Brazil:	55-11-813-3044
Chile:	562-232-8966
Colombia:	571-256-6529
Costa Rica:	506-234-6666
Mexico:	535-395-6532
Venezuela:	582-241-0433

Australia

Chatswood:	61-2-415-9000

Europe

France:	33-1-4087-3737 or 33-1-4792-0113
Germany:	49-211-560-30
Italy:	39-2-26233
Spain:	34-3-582-1500
UK:	44-442-61144 (includes Middle East) or 44-442-227-355 (includes Africa)

Asia

Hong Kong:	852-489-9119
Singapore:	65-533-0477
Taiwan:	886-2-717-7360

E

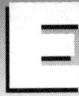

Ergo Computing, Inc.

- ▶ Brick–16 MHz 80386SX-based desktop computer system
- ▶ DPM 16/32 (DPMX)–DOS extender with DPMI host and client mode
- ▶ Nifty Fifty–50 MHz 486DX2 color LCD notebook computer
- ▶ Notebrick–33 MHz 80486-based notebook computer
- ▶ OS/286 Developer's Kit–DOS extender
- ▶ OS/286 DPMI Developer's Kit
- ▶ OS/386 Developer's Kit–DOS extender
- ▶ OS/386 DPMI Developer's Kit
- ▶ Powerbrick–486 portable computer
- ▶ Thinbrick–486 notebook computer

Voice, Standard Support: 508-535-7510 or 800-633-1922

Fax Support: 508-535-7512

Automated Fax-Back Support: 800-723-0778

Online Computer Support

 Computer Support via Ergo Computing's BBS Phone: 508-535-7228

E-ware

- ▶ Winsense

Voice, Standard Support: 603-644-5555
 Standard support is available 9 AM to 5:30 PM, Eastern Time, Monday to Friday.

Fax Support: 603-497-5638

Online Computer Support

 Computer Support via E-ware's BBS: 603-6444-5556

Express Systems

- ▶ Power Launcher
- ▶ Windows Express
- ▶ FirstApps
- ▶ Icon Designer

Voice, Standard Support: 206-728-8300
Standard support is available 8 AM to 5 PM, Pacific Time, Monday to Friday. Technical support for these products is free to registered users.

Fax Support: 206-728-8301

Online Computer Support

Computer Support via Express Systems' BBS: 206-728-8302

CompuServe: GO WINAPA–under hDC

America OnLine: Windows Vendors–hdctech

World Wide Web: A server containing information on Express Systems, software license metering, and management, technical information on Express Meter and hDC retail products is coming soon.

F

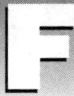

Fantazia Concepts, Inc.

▶ Font Elegance–Truetype and Geoworks fonts on CD-ROM
▶ Icons, Wallpaper, And More for Windows–CD-ROM
▶ World Class Fonts–Truetype and Geoworks fonts on CD-ROM

Voice, Standard Support: 216-951-5666 or 800-951-0877

Fax Support: 216-951-9241

Online Computer Support

> *America OnLine:* FantaziaC

Farallon Computing

Voice, Standard Support: 510-814-5000
Standard support is available 6 AM to 5:30 PM, Pacific Time, Monday to Friday.

Fax Support: 510-814-5023

Online Computer Support

> *Internet:* techsports@farallon.com
>
> *AppleLink:* TECHSPORTS
>
> *CompuServe:* 75410.2702
>
> *America OnLine:* Farallon
>
> *E-World:* Farallon50
>
> *World Wide Web:* Farallon has a World Wide Web server full of product and company information and technical notes. You can reach it at http://www.farallon.com. Mosaic or some other WWW-compatible browser is required.

Federated Telecommunications Corp.

▶ Virtual Monitors 3.0

Online Computer Support

  CompuServe: 75300,3712
  Baseline Publishing message section on in
  WINVEND.
  Type: GO BASELINE

  Internet: 75300.3712@CompuServe.com

Firefly Software Corp.

▶ PhotoGenix–photographic screensaver for
  Windows
▶ PhotoGenix Professional Edition–photographic
  screensaver

Voice, Standard Support: 516-935-7060 or
  800-224-2778

Fax Support: 516-932-7905

Online Computer Support

  CompuServe: 73354,2672

First Floor, Inc.

  First Floor, Inc. provides free technical support to
  all purchasers of Network Central.

Voice, Standard Support: 415-968-1135

Fax Support: 415-968-1193

Online Computer Support

  Computer Support via FirstFloor's BBS: 415-968-0428

  CompuServe: Type: GO FIRSTFLOOR

  Internet: ncentral-support@firstfloor.COM

  Anonymous ftp: ftp.firstfloor.COM

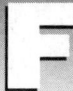

Foley Hi-Tech Systems

▶ ExtraDOS ToolBox–a collection of over 50 DOS utilities
▶ TurboBAT–batch file compiler
▶ CleanUp for Windows–finds and removes duplicate files
▶ Safety Disk–system backup and recovery program

Voice, Standard Support: 415-882-1730

Fax Support: 415-882-1733

Online Computer Support

Computer Support via Foley's BBS: 415-882-1735

CompuServe: 71333,3657
PCSVENB Section/Library 13

Fostex Corp. of America

▶ Professional audio recording and editing products for film, broadcast TV and radio, music, and the spoken-word industries.

Voice, Standard Support: 800-7-FOSTEX or 310-921-1112
800-8-FOSTEX (for Digital Audio Workstation Support only)
Fostex has an onsite Factory Service Center that can be reached from 7 AM to 5 PM, Pacific Time. Technical Support for all Fostex products, except the Digital Audio Workstation product line, is handled at the California office: 1-800-7-FOSTEX.

Customers using the Foundation 2000 digital Recorder, Editor, and Mixer and the associated product line can call the East Coast office for Customer and Product Applications Support at 1-800-8-FOSTEX. No additional charges beyond local phone company toll charges are required.

Fostex Corp. of America

Calls can be made to this office between the hours of 8:30 AM and 11 PM, Eastern Time.

Fax Support: 310-802-1964

Online Computer Support

CompuServe: Type: GO FOSTEX

☎ If you prefer, Fostex also can be contacted via the Performing Artist Network (PAN) for any technical questions and issues.

Frobozz Magic Software Company

▶ Icon Heaven, version 1.03

Online Computer Support

CompuServe: 75170,1045
Type: GO SWREG

Internet: pvk@acm.org

Fidonet: 2:285/324.10

OS2NET: 81:431/41.10

☎ Registration includes the right to lifetime upgrades and free support on an "as is" basis

Funk Software, Inc.

▶ Allways–print enhancer for 1-2-3
▶ Allways for Symphony
▶ Appmeter–application-metering program for networks
▶ Formula Editor–Lotus 1-2-3 add-in utility
▶ Inword–Lotus 1-2-3 add-in
▶ Noteworthy–cell annotation and documentation software
▶ P.D.Queue–add-in print spooler for 1-2-3 and Symphony
▶ Proxy–multi-remote control utility for Windows

- ▶ Remote Control–remotely control other PCs via a network
- ▶ Sideways–spreadsheet print utility
- ▶ Wanderlink–remote access software for NetWare networks
- ▶ Worksheet Utilities–Lotus 1-2-3 add-in

Voice, Standard Support: 617-497-6339 or 800-828-4146

Fax Support: 800-828-4146

Future Domain Corp.

- ▶ FDU-CD–compact disc device driver
- ▶ FDU-FD–floppy driver
- ▶ FDU-OS/2–fixed disk device driver for SCSI host board
- ▶ Future/CAM for Windows–SCSI multitasking for Windows
- ▶ MCS-350–8-bit MCA SCSI host adapter board
- ▶ MCS-600–ISA and MCA SCSI host adapter boards
- ▶ MCS-700–MCA SCSI host adapter board
- ▶ SCSI2GO–PCMCIA SCSI interface card
- ▶ TMC-1600 Series–16-bit ISA SCSI host adapter boards
- ▶ TMC-1760–16-bit EISA SCSI bus host adapter board
- ▶ TMC-1790–16-bit EISA SCSI bus host adapter with 16-bit BIOS
- ▶ TMC-3260–PCI bus SCSI-2 adapter board with boot ROM
- ▶ TMC-3260MEX–ecomonical PCI bus SCSI-2 adapter board
- ▶ TMC-7000EX Bus Master–EISA SCSI host adapter board
- ▶ TMC-800 Series–8-bit PC/AT SCSI host adapter board

Future Domain Corp.

Voice, Standard Support: 714-253-0440

Online Computer Support

> *Computer Support via Future Domain's BBS Phone:* 714-253-0432

FutureSoft Engineering

- ▶ Plus/Fax–Terminal Plus with Eclipse Fax
- ▶ DynaComm Async–asynchronous terminal emulation for Windows with a network
- ▶ DynaComm Elite–3270 DFT mode terminal emulator
- ▶ DynaComm/OpenConnect TN3270–3270 terminal emulation via TCP/IP
- ▶ DynaComm/Openconnect 5250–5250 terminal emulation via TCP/IP

Voice, Standard Support: 713-496-9400 or 713-588-6868

Fax Support: 713-496-1090

Online Computer Support

> *Computer Support via FutureSoft's BBS:* 713-588-6870
>
> *CompuServe:* 76702,755
>
> *Internet:* support@fse.com

Futurus Corp.

Voice, Standard Support: 404-825-0379
Standard support is available 8:30 AM to 6 PM, Eastern Time, Monday to Friday.

Fax Support: 404-392-9313

Online Computer Support

> *Computer Support via Futurus' BBS:* 404-242-7857
>
> *CompuServe:* GO FUTURUS
>
> *Internet:* tech@futurus.com

Special Information

In addition, Futurus offers priority 800 support for large accounts. Please be at your computer when calling our technical support staff to give them the best opportunity to serve you.

Galacticomm, Inc.

▶ Major BBS software

Voice, Standard Support: 305-321-2404
Standard support is available 8:30 AM to 6 PM,
Eastern Time, Monday to Friday. Unlimited
phone support, within reason, to all registered
owners and to prospects evaluating our software.

☎ 24-hour E-mail support. All E-mail generally is
answered within 24 hours of receipt. Includes
Internet and other network mail.

Online Computer Support
Demo System–Technical Support

MajorNET: Tech Support@GCM

Internet: support@gcomm.com

CompuServe: 72662,3341

America OnLine: GcommSuprt
Espanol–Soporte Tecnico

Demo System–SYSOPS and SUPPORT forums

MajorNET: SYSOPS and SUPPORT forums

Internet: alt.bbs.majorbbs and
comp.bbs.majorbbs

CompuServe: PCSVENJ forum, section 14

Third Party Services: Developer Support

Demo System–Developer

Internet: develop@gcomm.com

Gamma Productions, Inc.

▶ Multilingual Scholar–foreign language word
processor
▶ Unitype Localization Kit for Windows

▶ Universe for Windows–foreign language educational software

Voice, Standard Support: 619-794-6399 or 800-974-2662

Fax Support: 619-794-7294

GammaLink

▶ CAD-Fax–PC-to-fax system for CAD users
▶ Gammafax Communications Software–OS/2 communications software
▶ Gammafax CP4/LSI broadcast fax board
▶ Gammafax CPD–9600bps answer-only LAN fax/modem board
▶ Gammafax Cpi–14.4Kbps network-ready fax/modem board
▶ Gammafax MLCP-4–14.4Kbps four-port fax boards
▶ Gammafax Programmer's Interface–C Programmer's toolkit
▶ Gammafax Xpi–9600bps network-ready fax/modem board
▶ Gammanet–network fax server
▶ Gammanet Windows–network fax server
▶ Gammapage–fax translation utility software

Voice, Standard Support: 408-744-1400 or 800-592-6300
Alternate Voice Support: 619-481-2881 or 203-978-1918

Fax Support: 415-744-1900
Alternate Fax Support: 619-481-5266 or 203-359-9203

Online Computer Support

Computer Support via GammaLink's BBS: 408-745-2216

GammaLink

Gateway Software, Inc.

- ► EVA–GEnie Telecom front-end software
- ► LISTICO–Windows icon display utility
- ► MYMIQ–update prices in MYM or MYMIC investment accounts
- ► Pro$tock–Prodigy stock market information utilities
- ► Promaster–investment software for use with Prodigy
- ► Proplus–general Prodigy utility package
- ► QMU–investment support software for Quicken and Prodigy users
- ► Yoursys–system information utility

Voice, Standard Support: 415-885-0593

Online Computer Support

   CompuServe: 73567,2755

General Software

- ► Booter Toolkit–build bootable demos and operating systems
- ► CodeProbe–software analyzer for DOS developers
- ► Device Driver SDK–for Embedded DOS
- ► Embedded BIOS–for nonstandard hardware/controllers
- ► Embedded DOS–realtime MS-DOS 3.31 clone
- ► EtherProbe–Ethernet network analyzer
- ► LANprobe–Ethernet network analyzer
- ► PRINTF for Assembly language
- ► Snooper–Ethernet protocol analyzer
- ► Utility SDK–for Embedded DOS

Voice, Standard Support: 206-391-4285 or 800-336-1166

Fax Support: 206-557-0736

Online Computer Support

Computer Support via General's BBS: 206-557-4227

Genoa Systems Corp.

- ▶ 1MB VGA 7860 graphics board
- ▶ 5000 Series SuperVGA graphics controller cards
- ▶ 6000 Series SuperVGA graphics controller cards
- ▶ AudioBahn–multimedia audio board with SCSI interface
- ▶ AudioBlitz Classic–8/16-bit audio board, record/playback
- ▶ AudioBlitz Stereo 16+–MPC2 compliant sound board
- ▶ AudioGraphix–multimedia board with 24-bit true color/16-bit audio
- ▶ Flickerfree SuperVGA graphics adapter
- ▶ FlickerFree Windows VGA 8800 graphics board with Scansafe
- ▶ Galaxy series of tape backup systems
- ▶ MultimediaVGA 7900 graphics board
- ▶ Phantom 32i model 8900VL-20–32-bit graphics accelerator board
- ▶ SuperEGA HiRes graphics adapter
- ▶ SuperXGA 9600 graphics adapter
- ▶ SysLink 3270VGA–3270 terminal emulation for Windows
- ▶ SysLink Ethernet
- ▶ VGA2TV–multimedia graphics board
- ▶ VGA2TV Pro–multimedia graphics board
- ▶ VideoBlitz–VESA/PCI local bus graphics adapters
- ▶ VideoMotion–video overlay/capture board
- ▶ WindowsVGA 24 VL–graphics board with VL-bus interface
- ▶ WindowsVGA 24+ VL–graphics board with VL-bus interface

Genoa Systems Corp.

▶ WindowsVGA 3000 Series Windows graphics
accelerator card

Voice, Standard Support: 408-432-9090 or
800-934-3662
Alternate Voice Support: 408-432-8324

Fax Support: 408-434-0997

Online Computer Support

Computer Support via Genoa's BBS: 408-943-1231
Alternate Information: 9600bps support modem
line
Alternate BBS: 408-943-1256

Global Village Comm.

▶ Teleport
▶ Powerport

Online Computer Support

America OnLine: Keyword: Global

CompuServe: 75300,3473
Type: GO GLOBAL

E-World: Global Village forum
Type: GO Global

AppleLink: Third Party Support area: GlobalVillage
globalvillag

Internet: techsupport@globalvillag.com
Newsgroups: comp.sys.mac.comm,
comp.sys.mac.hardware

Prodigy: FMJM51A

☎ OneNet conferences (accessible from ours and
other BBSs) include Modems, Mac Hardware,
PowerBook, and Global Village Support. For the
fastest response and the best level of OnLine
service, we recommend direct E-mail instead of
the forums.

Global Village Comm.

GoldDisk

▶ Anim. Works, Video Dir.

Voice, Standard Support: 416-602-4000
  Amiga Tech: 416-602-4357
  IBM Tech: 416-602-5292
  Mac Tech: 416-602-0395

Fax Support: 416-602-0393

Online Computer Support

  Computer Support via GoldDisk's BBS: 416-602-7534

  Internet: Tech@GoldDisk.Com

  CompuServe: 75300,3433

Graphical Bytes, Inc.

▶ Shareware from Enis Morgan
▶ CD Mini-Player for Windows–software to play music via CD-ROM drive
▶ CD Player for Windows–software to play music via CD-ROM drive

Voice, Standard Support: 516-775-4714 or 800-MINI-CD

Graphsoft

Standard support is available 9 AM to 5:30 PM, Eastern Time, Monday to Friday. Registered users have unlimited access for 18 months from the time of purchase. Graphsoft encourages their users to communicate by fax.

Fax Support: 410-290-5114
Faxes are useful for complex questions, like those involving macro code.

Online Computer Support

  CompuServe: 72662,1320

America OnLine: search for MCadTech

AppleLink: D 0313

Internet: via our America OnLine
(MCadTech@aol.com), AppleLink
(D 0313@applelink.com) or CIS
(72662,1320@cis.com) addresses. Questions
posted by fax or E-mail will be answered within
one working day.

Great Lakes Software, Inc.

▶ GLS-Presto

Voice, Standard Support: 219-481-5809
Great Lakes Software provides free support for 90
days via telephone. After 90 days, support other
than CompuServe is provided for a fee.

Online Computer Support

CompuServe: 73762,114

Gulick

▶ The "Fly XXX" Series for Flight Simulator

Phone: 1-407-642-7704

Online Computer Support

CompuServe: 71241,321

Hayes Microcomputer

▶ Modems

Voice, Standard Support: 404-441-1617

Fax Support: 404-449-0087
    Fax Response (fax on demand): 800-HAYESFX

Online Computer Support
    Computer Support via Hayes' BBS: 404-446-6336
    Internet: Tech_Support@Hayes.Com
    CompuServe: Go HayForum
    GEnie: Go HayForum

☎ We also monitor and answer questions on Ilink, SmartNet, and FIDOnet. All support currently is free.

Special Information
    In addition to the previous information, we also have outlying offices in the UK and Hong Kong for our international offices.

HelgaSoft

▶ Accuboard–append/save Windows clipboard text
▶ Maxess Lite–Access/Procomm online database Software

Online Computer Support
    CompuServe: 72103,1062

Helix Software Company, Inc.

Voice, Standard Support: 718-392-3735
    Standard support is available 9:30 AM to 5 PM, Eastern Time, Monday to Friday.

Fax Support: 718-392-4212

Online Computer Support

Computer Support via Helix's BBS: 718-392-4054

CompuServe: GO HELIXS forum in PCSVENG

Special Information

Priority and toll-free support are available to corporate customers on a fee and/or site-license basis.

Helpful Programs, Inc. (HPI)

▶ hpiOMNI for DOS–installation utility
▶ Instalit–Software installation utility
▶ Instalit DOS Multi-Lingual
▶ Instalit for Windows
▶ PORTALS–presentation toolkit

Voice, Standard Support: 205-880-8782

Fax Support: 205-880-8782 or 800-448-4154

Hewlett-Packard

Voice, Standard Support: 916-785-2688

Standard support is available 8 AM to 5 PM, Pacific Time, Monday and Tuesday through Friday; 8 AM to 3 PM, Wednesday (closed early for meetings).

Fax Support: 916-785-3090

Online Computer Support

Computer Support via Hewlett-Packard's BBS: 916-785-2689

CompuServe: Type: GO HPSYS

Internet:
Type: support@support.mayfield.hp.com (send in the text portion of the message).

Hilbert Computing

▶ Chron v4.0 (for OS/2)

Voice, Standard Support: 913-780-5051

Fax Support: 913-829-2450

Online Computer Support

CompuServe: 73457,365
OS2AVEND Lib 1

Hilgraeve, Inc.

▶ HyperAccess–communications software
▶ HyperAccess for Windows–communications software
▶ HyperCopy–antivirus software utility
▶ HyperProtocol
▶ KopyKat Remote Control Software for OS/2

Voice, Standard Support: 313-243-0576 or 800-826-2760

Fax Support: 313-243-0645

Online Computer Support

Computer Support via Hilgraeve's BBS: 313-243-5915

HockWare

▶ VisPro/REXX
▶ VisPro/C++
▶ VisPro/C
▶ Data Entry Object Pack for VisPro/REXX

Voice, Standard Support: 919-380-0616

Fax Support: 919-380-0757

Online Computer Support

CompuServe: 71333,3226

Internet: hockware@vnet.net

Hook and Gresseth Software (H+G Software)

▶ Explosiv Screen Saver–shareware utility for DOS and Windows

Voice, Standard Support: 604-277-8914
   Alternate Voice Support: 604-738-0045

Online Computer Support

   CompuServe: 73042,3653

   Internet: gresseth@ucs.ubc.ca

Horizons Technology, Inc.

▶ Fuzzy Search Engine–text search tool for Windows NT
▶ Fuzzy Search Engine Developer's Kit
▶ LANAuditor–software for tracking network resources
▶ LANshadow–network server data mirroring software
▶ LANtrack–network performance data monitoring software
▶ LANtrail–network security and monitoring software
▶ Micro Auditor–hardware inventory for nonnetworked PCs
▶ Power!Control–simple, flexible DOS shell
▶ Power!Search–full text search tool
▶ Power!Search Professional for Windows NT–full text search tool
▶ Power!Video: Executive–true-motion digital video
▶ Power!Video: Producer–true-motion digital video
▶ Sure!Maps–map collection on CD-ROM

Voice, Standard Support: 619-292-8320 or 800-828-3808

Fax Support: 619-292-9439

Howling Dog Systems

Voice, Standard Support: 613-599-7927

Our tech support is free to registered customers (return of warranty card with serial number required).

Online Computer Support

CompuServe: 71333,2166
GO HOWLING

HPS

▶ Tigers On the Prowl
▶ Aide De Camp
▶ Point Of Attack

Voice, Standard Support: 408-554-8381

Fax Support: 408-241-6886

Online Computer Support

Computer Support via HPS BBS:
GEnie
CServe
Prodigy

Hyperkinetix, Inc.

▶ Builder

Voice, Standard Support: 714-573-2260

Online Computer Support

Computer Support via Hyperkinetix's BBS: 714-573-3993

IBM

Product and Service Access: 800-426-4968

Services and Support: 800-426-7378 (hardware
assistance)
800-237-5511 (software assistance)

Online Computer Support

Internet:
For IBM Universal (URL) http://www.ibm.com/
IBMLink gopher.ibmlink.ibm.com

Imageline, Inc.

▶ ActionPak–animations/sprites/frames for
Storyboard Live!
▶ Holiday Clips–clipart collection
▶ PicturePak Fun Pak–clipart collection
▶ PicturePak Pro–clipart collection for Windows
▶ PicturePak Super Pak–clipart collection
▶ PicturePak: Executive and Management–clipart
collection
▶ PicturePak: Holiday Clips–clipart collection
▶ PicturePak: Office Clips–clipart collection
▶ PicturePak: Sales and Marketing–clipart collection
▶ PicturePak: Technology–clipart collection
▶ PicturePak: U.S. Maps–clipart collection
▶ Typestyles II–typeface collection
▶ ValuePak–clipart collection
▶ ValuePak for Windows–clipart collection

Voice, Standard Support: 804-644-0766
Alternate Voice Support: 305-422-5555

Fax Support: 804-644-0769
Alternate Fax Support: 305-422-5577

Impact Software, Inc.

▶ Impact Formatted Entryfields–window class for OS/2

Voice, Standard Support: 818-879-5592 or 800-676-9390

Fax Support: 818-879-5593

Online Computer Support

Computer Support via Impact's BBS: 818-879-7405

Infinite Technologies

▶ CastAway!–NetWare message broadcast
▶ ExpressIT! Electronic Mail
▶ ExpressIT! for OS/2–electronic mail
▶ ExpressIT! for Windows–electronic mail
▶ ExpressIT! Remote–remote electronic mail
▶ ExpressIT! Remote for Windows–remote E-mail
▶ ForwardIT!–multipurpose MHS forwarding agent
▶ I-Queue–pop-up NetWare capture utility
▶ LockIT!–lock local workstation after inactive period
▶ Login with TSRs
▶ MHS Librarian!–remote file retrieval via MHS
▶ MHS Notify!–inbound MHS mail notification
▶ MHS Scheduler!–electronic mail connection control
▶ MHSB+
▶ MhsQ!–MHS interface to NetWare print queues
▶ NETERR–NetWare utilities to reboot PC on NetWare abort err
▶ OnCall!–chat utility for Novell NetWare
▶ PageIT!–E-mail gateway interface for pagers
▶ PopIT!–turn almost any program into pop-up utility
▶ SendIT!–send MHS E-mail messages from batch files

Voice, Standard Support: 410-363-1097
> Standard support is available 9 AM to 6 PM, Eastern Time, Monday to Friday. Thirty-day evaluation products and purchased products are serviced by Infinite's responsive Technical Support Representatives. You receive free, unlimited technical support for information and answers to your questions.

FAX Support: 410-363-0846 or 410-363-3779

Online Computer Support

> *CompuServe:* 73270,405
> MHS:SUPPORT @ INFINITE

> *MHS Direct:* 410-363-1210

> *NHUB:* INFINITE

> *Internet:* Infinite.ihub.com

> *World Wide Web:* www.ihub.com

> *FTP:* ftp.ihub.com
> Please be ready to provide the following information:

1. Product and version number
2. Type of network (Novell or peer-to-peer) and version number
3. Error message, if any
4. Version of MHS, if any
5. Command line options used, if any

Special Information
> Infinite suggests the following forums if you are interested in additional technical information on network communications in an MHS environment:

CompuServe: Type: GO INFINITE to reach the Infinite Technologies section of the Novell vendor forum.

The Infinite Loop: We encourage you to subscribe to our discussion list, which is called The Infinite Loop. To subscribe, send a message via CompuServe or NHUB to Library @ Infinite with a subject line of SUBSCRIBE.

Informative Graphics Corp.

Voice, Standard Support: 602-971-6061

Fax Support: 602-971-1714

Online Computer Support

Computer Support via IGC's BBS: 602-971-6079
This BBS supports baud rates up to 14.4Kbps and operates 24 hours a day, 7 days a week.

Internet: info@infograph.com

CompuServe: Type: GO IGCCORP

CompuServe: 72662,3001

Inmagic, Inc.

► VAX/VMS versions of INMAGIC and SearchMAGIC
► INMAGIC Plus
► INMAGIC Image
► SearchMAGIC Plus
► INMAGIC Scan
► Standalone IMPORT
► Legal Guide
► Library Guide
► MARC Adaptor
► MULTI Adaptor
► Document Adaptor
► PowerPack

Voice, Standard Support: 617-938-4442

Standard support is available 8:30 AM to 5:30 PM, Eastern Time, Monday to Friday. However, you can send a fax or leave voice mail 24 hours a day, and a technical support representative will call you.

Phone support is provided at no charge to people who have purchased an Inmagic product within the last 45 days or who recently have received TestMAGIC or a Guided Tour. After that period, annual phone support contracts are available at $300 in the U.S.

Technical support, application customization, and training also are available from Inmagic, Inc.'s extensive network of value-added resellers. Outside the U.S., phone support is provided by local dealers at various charges.

Fax Support: 617-938-6393

Online Computer Support

Internet: inmagic@netcom
Inmagic, Inc. monitors the comp.databases USENET newsgroup and will respond to any message with INMAGIC in the Subject.

CompuServe: 71333,105

Forums: To contact other INMAGIC users as well as Inmagic, Inc., users can send messages to either our CompuServe Forum or to the comp.databases USENET newsgroup on the Internet.

CompuServe: PCSVENB forum in section 15
Type: GO INMAGIC

Libraries:
Inmagic, Inc. also maintains libraries on both CompuServe and the Internet. These libraries

include product maintenance releases, freeware utilities, and helpful fact sheets. Both libraries include a file called TITLES.TXT, listing and describing all the files available in the library.

Internet FTP library instructions:

1. Type "ftp ftp.netcom.com" (yes, you really need both "ftp").

2. Login as "anonymous." Example:
   Name (stuff in parentheses): anonymous

3. Type your E-mail address in response to the password prompt. Example:
   Password: lisa@mit.edu

4. Type "cd pub/inmagic" at the ftp> prompt. Example:
   ftp> cd pub/inmagic

CompuServe library instructions:
Type: GO INMAGIC. If you have not yet joined the PCSVENB/INMAGIC forum, type: JOIN. Type: LIB 15.

BBS/Internet LISTSERV:
An INMAGIC user, Dan Wendling at NARIC, maintains a LISTSERV to discuss issues related to making INMAGIC databases available via BBS and the Internet. This LISTSERV should not be used to discuss general INMAGIC issues.

To subscribe to the INMAGIC-ONLINE LISTSERV, send a message with no subject to listserv@knowledgework.com with SUBSCRIBE INMAGIC-ONLINE FIRSTNAME LASTNAME in the body of the message.

Inmagic, Inc.

Special Information
Clients who purchase an annual support contract automatically receive product maintenance releases by mail.

Newsletter
Clients who return the registration card included with their software receive the INMAGIC newsletter (approximately quarterly) at no charge. The newsletter includes product announcements, helpful tips and techniques, articles written by users, training schedules and more.

Inmark Development Corp.

- ▶ Inmark Open Windows
- ▶ Market Maker 4 Windows–technical analysis and charting
- ▶ QuotChart–stock charting and technical analysis
- ▶ QuotData–real-time securities information
- ▶ QuotTerm–real-time securities display
- ▶ Zapp for DOS/Windows–application development framework
- ▶ Zapp for Windows NT–application development framework

Voice, Standard Support: 415-691-9000 or 800-346-6275
Alternate Voice Support: 212-406-2299

Fax Support: 415-691-9099
Alternate Fax Support: 212-571-6523

Online Computer Support

Computer Support via Inmark's BBS: 415-691-9990

CompuServe: 70550, 2570

BIX: inmark

Internet: sales@inmark.com

L

Instant Replay Corp.

- ▶ Carets & Cursors–shareware mouse pointers and cursors
- ▶ Instant Replay Professional–multimedia system manager
- ▶ NoBlink–no blinking cursor utility
- ▶ Visual FX–special effects tool for Windows programmers

Voice, Standard Support: 801-272-0671, 800-388-8086

Fax Support: 801-634-1054

Online Computer Support

  Computer Support via Instant's BBS: 801-272-0675

Inset

Voice, Standard Support: 203-775-5634
  Standard support is available 9 AM to 5 PM, Eastern Time, Monday through Friday. Inset asks that before you call or fax technical support, you have the following:

  Windows 3.1 or later in standard or enhanced mode.
  Sufficient disk space.
  Available system resources above 25%.

  When you do call or fax, please know the following:

  HiJaak Graphics Suite serial and version number
  Computer make and model
  Detailed description of the problem, including exact wording of any error message

Fax Support: 203-775-5634

TDD Support: Call a Support Specialist through the BBS number.

Inset

Online Computer Support

Computer Support via Inset's BBS: 203-740-0063

CompuServe: Type: GO INSET

Intergalactic Development, Inc.

- ▶ UMS: The Universal Military Simulator
- ▶ UMS II: Nations at War
- ▶ The War College

Voice, Standard Support: 319-323-5293
Standard support is available 10 AM to 10 PM,
Central Time, Monday to Thursday, and 10 AM
to 8 PM, Friday, and noon to 8 PM, Saturday.

Fax Support: 319-323-0407

Online Computer Support

Internet: Ezra @ Intergalactic

Invisible Software, Inc.

- ▶ Invisible EMS–8MB LIM 4.0 expanded memory
  board
- ▶ Invisible Ethernet 2000TP–interface board
- ▶ Invisible Ethernet 3200–interface board
- ▶ Invisible Ethernet NET/30
- ▶ Invisible NET Control–remote-control program
- ▶ Invisible Network
- ▶ Invisible RAM–DOS memory extension
- ▶ InvisibleLAN–network operating system (was
  NET/30)
- ▶ InvisibleLAN for Windows–networking software
  (was NET/30)
- ▶ Thruport Ethernet Pocket Adapter
- ▶ Ultra–network operating system

Voice, Standard Support: 415-570-5967 or
800-982-2962
Alternate Voice Support: 407-260-5200

Fax Support: 415-570-6017
   Alternate Fax Support: 407-260-1841

Online Computer Support

   Computer Support via Invisible's BBS: 415-345-5509

InVision Systems Corp.

▶ InVision Video Conferencing for Windows
▶ VisionGraphics for Windows–graphical
   communications software

Voice, Standard Support: 703-506-0094 or
   800-284-3364

Fax Support: 703-506-0098

Online Computer Support

   CompuServe: 72002,1677

   Internet: info@invision.com

Iomega

▶ Tape backups

Voice, Standard Support: 800-456-5522
   24-hour support for sales and technical questions.
   Customer Service-Bernoulli/DOS: 801-629-7610
   Customer Service-Bernoulli/Mac: 801-629-7620
   Customer Service-Tape250: 801-778-3010

FaxBack: 801-778-5763

Online Computer Support

   Computer Support via Iomega's BBS: 801-394-9819

   CompuServe: PCSVENE and MACCVEN forums

   America OnLine: Keyword: IOMEGA

   Internet: info@iomega.com

JASC

Voice, Standard Support: 612-930-9171

Fax Support: 612-930-9172

Online Computer Support

Computer Support via JASC's BBS: 612-930-3516

CompuServe:
GO WINAPCS, Section 19–JASC, Inc.

America OnLine:
Graphics Forum, OnLine Graphics Software,
Paint Shop Pro Area

Internet:
jasc@winternet.com

JLCooper Electronics

▶ Control products
▶ Mixing console automation systems
▶ Synchronizers
▶ Midi and computer peripherals for professional
audio, video, and multimedia markets

Voice, Standard Support: 310-822-2252 or 310-306-4131
Standard support is available 8 AM to 5 PM,
Pacific Time, Monday to Friday.

Fax Support: 310-822-2252

Online Computer Support

CompuServe: 75300,1373

Kayman Software

► KUtils–set of utility programs for Windows
► Pendulous–shareware game for Windows
► Screen Play–Windows screen saver

Voice, Standard Support: 708-837-0320

Online Computer Support

  CompuServe: 73447,1114

KIDASA Software, Inc.

► Milestones, Etc.–a Gantt chart/scheduling
  program for Windows

Voice, Standard Support: 512-328-0168
  Standard support is available 9 AM to 5 PM,
  Central Time, Monday to Friday. After-hours
  callers can leave a message on voice mail.

Fax Support: 512-328-0247

Online Computer Support

  CompuServe: 76702,1305
  KIDASA section (section 9) of the WINAPB
  forum.

Kingston Technology Corp.

► Wide assortment of memory and CPU upgrade
  boards
► 486/Now! processor upgrades
► AST Systems memory upgrade kits
► AT&T Personal Workstation memory upgrades
► Canon printer memory boards
► Compaq SystemPro and DeskPro memory
  upgrades
► Data Express–removable media data storage
► Data Express Junior (DE50)–removable hard disk
  drive

Kingston Technology Corp.

- Data Keeper–8GB SCSI interface tape drive
- Data Traveler, The–portable parallel port hard disk package
- DataCard–memory upgrade cards for PS/2 systems
- Epson Equity Series and EPL 6000 Laser printer memory upgrades
- Ethernet Pocket LAN adapter
- EtheRx 10BASE-T KNE2100T–network interface card
- EtheRx 10BASE2 KNE2102–network interface card
- EtheRx 2-in-1 KNE2121–combination network interface card
- EtheRx 2000 plus triple interface–Ethernet adapter
- EtheRx KNE-3233–32-bit Ethernet adapter
- EtheRx PCMCIA LAN adapters
- EtheRx Pocket LAN adapter
- HP Laser printer and Vectra memory boards, modules, etc.
- IBM PS/2 and Laser printer Memory Boards
- MCMaster–CPU upgrades for 386 MCA systems
- NEC PowerMate and ProSpeed memory upgrades
- Okidata Printer memory upgrades
- SLC/Now! processor upgrades
- SX/Now!–processor upgrade for 286 systems
- SX/Now!–processor upgrades
- TokenRx dual interface adapter card (KTRMC 16/4)
- Toshiba portable computer memory cards and modules
- ViewRx–graphics accelerator board
- ViewRX VGA–Windows accelerator Board (KWT5186)
- Zenith Data Systems memory upgrades, cards, etc.

Kingston Technology Corp.

Voice, Standard Support: 714-435-2600 or 800-835-6575
Alternate Voice Support: 714-435-2639

Fax Support: 714-435-2699

Online Computer Support

Computer Support via Kingston's BBS: 714-435-2636

Internet: E-mail address: techsupport@kingston.com

Knacks

Voice, Standard Support: 908-530-0262
Standard support is available 9 AM to 5 PM, Eastern Time, Monday to Friday.

Fax Support: 908-741-0972
Support is free to all registered users.

Online Computer Support

CompuServe: 74431,3575
Type: GO KNACKS

Knowledge Garden, Inc.

▶ KPWin++–Windows application development environment that generates C++ code
▶ KPWin SQLKIT–client/ server development
▶ WRAP–on-the-fly data compression

Voice, Standard Support: 516-862-0600
Knowledge Garden, Inc. offers free support for the first 60 days or 15 calls. After this, they offer annual ($395), lifetime ($595), commercial ($3995), and pay-by-use ($15) support plans.

Fax Support: 516-862-0644

Knowledge Garden, Inc.

Online Computer Support

CompuServe: 76004,1603
WINAPB Section 15, by phone

Worldwide Support

Europe
Voice, Standard Support: 44-753-710500
Fax Support: 44-753-790755

KnowledgePoint Software

▶ Descriptions Now!–write custom job descriptions
▶ Performance Now!–create performance appraisals
▶ Performance Now! for Windows–create performance appraisals
▶ Personnel Policy Expert–create employee handbooks
▶ Policies Now!–employee handbook generation

Voice, Standard Support: 707-762-0333 or 800-727-1133

Fax Support: 707-762-0802

KnowledgeWare, Inc.

▶ Accesspoint–DB2/SQL queries and reports for Windows NT
▶ Application Development Workbench (ADW)–CASE tool
▶ ClearAccess–graphical database access tool for Windows
▶ ClearManager–graphical database management tool for Windows
▶ Flashpoint–GUI development tool
▶ IEW/Analysis Workstation
▶ IEW/CWS–COBOL applications generator
▶ IEW/Planning Workstation

KnowledgePoint Software

- ► Information Engineering Workbench–CASE tool
- ► MAXIM–business process reengineering tool for Windows
- ► NorthStar–software reengineering tool for Windows developers
- ► ObjecView–client/server application development tool
- ► ObjecView Desktop–client/server application development tool

Voice, Standard Support: 404-231-8575, 800-444-8575, or 800-344-2662

Fax Support: 404-399-5755

Korenthal Associates, Inc.

- ► 4Print V4.16–HP LaserJet/DeskJet landscape printing utility
- ► PhDbase III V3.21–full-text/fuzzy search library for FoxPro

Voice, Standard Support: 212-242-1790

Fax Support: 212-242-2599

Online Computer Support

> *CompuServe:* 76004,2605
> Type: GO KORENTHAL (same as PCSVENB Section 3)

LAB Tech

Voice, Standard Support: 508-657-5910

On purchase of new product, 90 days of support are free. After that, a yearly support contract is required.

Fax Support: 508-694-1091

Online Computer Support

Computer Support via LAB Tech's BBS: 508-988-9292
This BBS is used mainly for uploads and downloads.
Name: VISION
Password: REALTIME

CompuServe: GO LABTECH

Landmark Research Int'l Corp.

▶ Kickstart–system diagnostics card
▶ Landmark DOS–Windows shell
▶ Landmark SysInfo–system analysis software
▶ Landmark System Speed Test–system performance test software
▶ PC Certify–diagnostic software package for end users
▶ PC Probe–system diagnostics and benchmarks
▶ SCSI Troubleshooter Toolbox, The–diagnostic software
▶ WinProbe–system diagnostics and benchmarks

Voice, Standard Support: 813-443-1331 or 800-683-6696

Fax Support: 813-443-6603

LANshark Systems, Inc.

▶ Electronic mail packages for Windows networks
▶ Network management packages

L

Voice, Standard Support: 614-866-5553

Standard support is available from 8 AM to 5 PM, Eastern Time, Monday to Friday.

Fax Support: 614-866-4877

Fax support is available during the standard support hours.

Online Computer Support

CompuServe: 72567,1151
GO MAIL

Internet: 72567.1151@compuserve.com

LaserMaster Corp.

▶ DisplayMaker Professional–large-format color printer
▶ DisplayMaster–large-format color printer/plotter
▶ GlassPage GP 1280–19-inch 1280×1024 monochrome display
▶ GrayScale 1280–outline font monitor
▶ LaserMaster 1000 Personal Typesetter–1,000 dpi
▶ LaserMaster 1200XL Personal Typesetter–1,200 dpi printer
▶ LaserMaster 400XL–400 dpi 11"×17" printer
▶ LaserMaster 80Q and 800/4–800×800 dpi laser printer
▶ LaserMaster Series III Professional Printer Controller
▶ LC2 Controller–add-on high-resolution printer controller
▶ LM-Page
▶ MaxWriter 1000kx–8-ppm laser printer
▶ PressMate–2,400 dpi 12"×26" film printer
▶ Unity 1200XL-O Plain Paper Typesetter–1,200 dpi, 12"×19"
▶ Unity 1200XL-T Plain Paper Typesetter–1,200 dpi, 11"×17"

LaserMaster Corp.

- ▶ Unity 1800 PM-R–1,800 dpi typesetting printer
- ▶ Unity 1800XL-O Plain Paper Typesetter–1,800 dpi, 12"×19.5"
- ▶ WinJet–Windows LaserJet printing speed-up utility packages
- ▶ WinPrinter 1000–1,000 dpi 4-ppm laser printer
- ▶ WinPrinter 400–4-ppm laser printer
- ▶ WinPrinter 600XL–600 dpi 11"×17" PostScript printer
- ▶ WinPrinter 800–PCL4 8-ppm laser printer

Voice, Standard Support: 612-944-9330 or 800-688-8342

Fax Support: 619-944-1244
Alternate Fax Support: 612-943-3737

Worldwide Support

Netherlands
Alternate Voice, Standard Support: 2503-22000
Alternate Fax Support: 2503-31240

LEAD Technologies, Inc.

- ▶ LEAD Compression Boards–add-in image compression boards
- ▶ LEADTools Conversion–subset of LEADTools best functions
- ▶ LEADTools Express–image file conversion and processing
- ▶ LEADTools NT–image file conversion and processing for WindowsNT
- ▶ LEADTools NT Express–image file conversion and processing
- ▶ LEADTools Professional–image file conversion and processing
- ▶ LEADTools Standard–image file conversion and processing

- ▶ LEADTools Visual Basic–image file conversion and processing
- ▶ LeadView–image file compression/decompression software
- ▶ LeadView/32 for Windows–image compression/decompression
- ▶ Pilot–basic shareware communications program

Voice, Standard Support: 704-549-5532 or 800-637-4699

Fax Support: 704-548-8161

Online Computer Support

> *Computer Support via Lead's BBS:* 704-549-9045

Lieberman and Associates Design and Engineering Group

- ▶ LAN Intensive Care Utilities for IBM LAN Server

Voice, Standard Support: 310-550-8575

Fax Support: 310-550-1152

Online Computer Support

> *Computer Support via Lieberman's BBS:* 310-550-5980
>
> *IBMLINK:* OS2BBS1—LANUTIL Forum (DEV2203)
>
> *CompuServe:* 76426,363
>
> *IBMMAIL/SNA:* USMVHLVH AT IBMMAIL
>
> *X.400:*
> G=LIEBEPL;S=LIEBERMAN;P=IBMMAIL;A=IBMX400;C=US
>
> *Internet:* 76426.363@CompuServe.com

Special Information

> We provide electronic updates via our BBS as well as CompuServe, IBMLINK, and Internet via the HOBBES ftp site (hobbes.nmsu.edu).

Lieberman and Associates Design

Lifestyle Software Group

- ▶ America Cooks American
- ▶ America Cooks Chinese
- ▶ America Cooks French
- ▶ America Cooks Mexican
- ▶ Betty Boop, The Complete Makeover For Your PC
- ▶ Betty Crocker's:
    40th Anniversary Cookbook–recipes on disk
    Eat and Lose Weight–recipes on disk
    Italian Cookbook–recipes on disk
    Low-Fat and Low-Cholesterol Cookbook–recipes
    Microwave Cookbook–recipes on disk
    New Boys and Girls Cookbook
    New Choices Cookbook for Windows
    Old-Fashioned Cookbook–recipes on disk
    Shortcut Cooking for the Smartcook–recipes
- ▶ Calmpute–biorhythmic information with Galvanic Skin sensor
- ▶ Canis–history, diseases, and first aid for dogs
- ▶ Casino Master–five casino games

Philip Lieberman of Lieberman and Associates

- ▶ LAN Intensive Care Utilities for IBM LAN Server

Philip Lieberman handles both the development and support of his product, which he says there is "nothing" he likes least about. The best thing, he says, is hearing how his product has saved people time and solved their problems with their LAN.

Lieberman has a B.A. degree in physics with minors in business and computer science. He is the owner of Lieberman and Associates and writes books and articles on OS/2 and real-time systems design.

Because his company works with a wide variety of hardware and software, Lieberman says that it some-

L

- ▶ Crossword Creator
- ▶ Diet Balancer
- ▶ DietPro for DOS–diet, nutrition, and exercise management software
- ▶ DietPro for Windows
- ▶ Five Weeks to Winning Bridge
- ▶ Fractal Paint Plus–image processing system
- ▶ Friendly Foods–vegetarian cooking package
- ▶ Fundwatch Plus–mutual fund and growth investment analysis
- ▶ Games Master for Windows–game collection
- ▶ Great Chefs, The–recipes and cooking tips
- ▶ High-Q–challenging multimedia games and exercises
- ▶ Hooked On Lottery–lottery analysis software
- ▶ Horizons: The Complete Genealogy System
- ▶ Lifestyle's Golf Companion–analysis/handicap, travel guide
- ▶ Micro Bridge Companion–three challenging Bridge programs

times is very difficult to pinpoint a single cause of a user's problem. The most common type of problem is how to setup the artificial intelligence rule-base for Lieberman's product.

He says users can help him arrive at a solution for their problems by reading the manual and preparing an assignment plan for their network. "Read books, take classes, try to learn the software inside and out," says Lieberman. "Don't read magazines like *PC Week* and *InfoWorld* for information, just entertainment."

To enable themselves to solve their own problems, Lieberman says that users should read the manual and try different scenarios: "Try to isolate the problem. Wait a day before calling and think about the problem."

- ▶ Micro Kitchen Companion–cooking assistant and recipes
- ▶ Micro Kitchen Companion for Windows–recipe management system
- ▶ Micro Wine Companion–wine cellar management system
- ▶ Micro Wine Companion for Windows
- ▶ Mr. Boston Official Micro Bartender's Guide–party planning
- ▶ Multimedia Pool–game program for Windows
- ▶ Multimedia Tarot for Windows
- ▶ Personal Portfolio Companion–money-management package
- ▶ Photo Family Tree, the Visual Genealogy System
- ▶ Puzzle Master–crossword puzzles
- ▶ Southern Living Cookbook Multimedia Edition for Windows, The
- ▶ Stereograms! for Windows–3D visualization tool
- ▶ Take Control of Your Cholesterol
- ▶ Timeless Hints from Heloise–household hints (Windows)
- ▶ Visions for Windows–astrology program
- ▶ Visions: The Complete Astrology System

Voice, Standard Support: 904-825-0220 or 800-289-1157

Fax Support: 904-825-0223

Lock 4 Software

- ▶ KbStuffer–an OS/2 full-screen keyboard buffer stuffer

Voice, Standard Support: 301-620-7142
Support by phone for registered users only.

Fax Support: 301-662-3909

L

Online Computer Support

> *Computer Support via Lock 4 Software's BBS:* 301-620-7138
>
> *FidoNet:* 1:109/742
>
> *OS2Net:* 81:125/301
>
> *CompuServe:* 72623,3533

Logitech, Inc.

- ▶ AudioMan–compact digital audio tool for Windows
- ▶ CatchWord Intelligent Character Recognition Software
- ▶ CatchWord Pro–OCR software for Windows
- ▶ CyberMan–3D interactive controller
- ▶ Dexxa Mouse
- ▶ Ergonomic Mouse
- ▶ Finesse–desktop publishing package
- ▶ First Mouse–three-button, entry-level, no-frills mouse
- ▶ First Trackball–value-priced stationary trackball
- ▶ FotoMan–digital camera with serial interface
- ▶ FotoMan Plus–upgraded digital camera with serial interface
- ▶ FotoTouch–image editing software for FotoMan and ScanMan 256
- ▶ HiREZ Bus Mouse
- ▶ Kidz Mouse–mouse controller for youngsters
- ▶ MindViewer–personality profiles and more
- ▶ Modern Art–electronic clip art library
- ▶ Modula OS/2 Compiler
- ▶ Modula-2 Compiler Pack
- ▶ Modula-2 Development System
- ▶ Modula-2 Toolkit
- ▶ Mouseman cordless radio mouse

Logitech, Inc.

- ▶ MouseMan high-resolution ergonomic mouse
- ▶ MouseMan Sensa line of personalized mouse controllers
- ▶ MovieMan video and audio capture board
- ▶ Multiscope Debugger–OS/2, multiple-language, CodeView compatible
- ▶ OmniPage Direct AnyFont OCR software for Logitech
- ▶ ScanMan–handheld 4" scanner
- ▶ ScanMan Color–24-bit color handheld scanner for Windows
- ▶ ScanMan EasyTouch–boardless 256 grayscale handheld scanner
- ▶ ScanMan Model 256–grayscale handheld scanner
- ▶ ScanMan Model 32–grayscale scanner
- ▶ ScanMan Plus–handheld scanner with improved case and rollers
- ▶ ScanMan PowerPage–256 grayscale full-page scanner
- ▶ Series 9 Mouse–extra high default resolution
- ▶ SoundMan 16–CD quality 16-bit stereo audio board
- ▶ SoundMan Games–8-bit stereo sound card for game players
- ▶ SoundMan Wave–16-bit stereo sound card with SCSI interface
- ▶ TrackMan Portable–mouse controller for portable computers
- ▶ Trackman Stationary Mouse–trackball controller
- ▶ TrackMan Voyager–trackball controller for portables
- ▶ WingMan–flight simulator joystick
- ▶ WingMan Extreme–flight simulator joystick

Voice, Standard Support: 510-795-8500 or 800-231-7717
Alternate Voice Support: 510-795-8100 (Product Support Hotline)

Fax Support: 510-792-8901
Alternate Fax Support: 800-245-0000

Online Computer Support

Computer Support via Logitech's BBS: 510-795-0408

Worldwide Support

Germany
Alternate Voice, Standard Support: 089588071
Alternate Fax Support: 0895808225

England
Alternate Voice, Standard Support: 0344-891-313
Alternate Fax Support: 0344-891-145

Switzerland
Alternate Voice, Standard Support: 218699656
Alternate Fax Support: 218699717

Looking Glass Software, Inc.

▶ Cheetah 3D–Windows-based rendering software
▶ HyperWrite–hypertext word processor for Windows
▶ MediaVerse–multimedia authoring software for Windows
▶ Raven3D–modeling and rendering software with walk thru capability
▶ RavenAudio–full visual control over Wave Audio
▶ RavenBase–cross platform database
▶ RavenDraw–object-oriented drawing program
▶ RavenSpeak–robust audio engine for multimedia applications
▶ RavenText–incorporate text objects in VB or C++ applications

- ▶ RavenWrite–incorporate hypermedia objects in VB/C++ applications
- ▶ ViperWrite–multimedia authoring software for Windows

Voice, Standard Support: 310-348-8240 or 800-859-8500

Fax Support: 310-348-9786

M

Mackie

Voice, Standard Support: 800-258-6883
Standard support is available 8 AM to 5 PM, Pacific Time, Monday to Friday.

Fax Support: 206-487-4337

Online Computer Support

Computer Support via Mackie's BBS: 206-488-4586

CompuServe: GO MACKIE

America OnLine: Type: GO MACKIE

Internet: technical.support@mackie.wa.com

Macromedia, Inc.

▶ Action! CD-ROM for Windows–2D animation software
▶ Action! for Windows–2D animation software
▶ AuthorWare Professional for Windows–multimedia authoring
▶ Business and Technology, ClipMedia 1–multimedia clipart
▶ Industry At Work, ClipMedia 2–Windows multimedia clips
▶ MacroModel–3D modeling program for Windows

Voice, Standard Support: 415-442-0200
800-288-8268

Fax Support: 415-442-0190

Madge Networks

▶ Token-ring products

Voice, Standard Support: 408-955-0700 or
800-876-2343
Standard support is available 6 AM to 6 PM, Pacific Time, Monday to Friday.

Fax Support: 408-955-0970
Faxback: 408-383-1002

Online Computer Support

Computer Support via Madge's BBS: 408-955-0262

Spaceworks BBS: 800-546-2500

CompuServe: 71333,2103
Type: GO MADGE
Section 16 of PCVENDORG forum

Internet:
71333.2103@COMPUSERVE.COM
SUPPORT@MADGE.COM

Worldwide Support
Madge Europe

Free phone numbers:
Austria: 0660-08366
Belgium: 0800-10485
Denmark: 800-17649
France: 05-90-82-50
Germany: 0130-868828
Italy: 1678-72092
Netherlands: 06022-7120
Norway: 800-11759
South Africa: 0800-991013
Spain: 900974412
Sweden: 020-793127
Switzerland(Fr): 155-6432
Switzerland(Gr): 155-1057
UK: 1345-125539

Fax Support: 44-1628-810-607

BBS: 44-1628-858-008
Hours of service 7 AM to 6 PM (GMT)

Madge Asia
Telephone: 852-593-9888

Madge Networks

Fax Support: 852-519-8022
BBS: 852-593-9829
Hours of service 9 AM to 6 PM, Monday to Friday

Madge Japan
Telephone: 81-3-5232-3281
Fax Support: 81-3-5232-3208
Hours of service 8 AM to 6 PM

Madge Singapore
Telephone: 65-538-8330
Fax Support: 65-538-8112
Hours of service 8 AM to 6 PM

Madge Oceania
Telephone: 61-2-256-2738
Fax Support: 61-2-256-2739
Hours of service 8 AM to 6 PM

☎ Should customers want to speak to a technical
support engineer out of hours, they are welcome
to call one of the other international offices who
will help or pass information to the relevant
regional office.

Magee Enterprises, Inc.

▶ Automenu/Treeview

Voice, Standard Support: 404-662-5387
Standard support is available 8:30 AM to 5:30 PM,
Eastern Time, Monday to Friday. Magee offers
free technical support to registered users of
Automenu and Network HQ.

Fax Support: 404-368-0719

Online Computer Support

Computer Support via Magee's BBS: 404-446-6650

Magee Enterprises, Inc.

Magnetic Music

▶ Texture–MIDI sequencer for MS-DOS
▶ MIDcat–a script-driven MIDI files processor

Currently, technical support for both products is available to registered users at no charge. This policy is subject to change.

Voice, Standard Support: 408-684-2654
Standard support is available 9 AM to 12:30 PM, Pacific Time, Monday to Thursday, and 10 AM to 2 PM Saturday.

Fax Support: 408-662-3134

Magus Software, Inc.

▶ PageTurner–PostScript file viewer

Voice, Standard Support: 415-940-1109

Online Computer Support

Internet: support@magus.com

CompuServe: OS2AVEN forum

Special Information

Our first-level technical support, such as answering questions and logging problem reports, is free. If a particular customer has special support needs that require more attention, then we negotiate a support contract for that customer.

Mallard Software, Inc.

▶ Air Traffic Controller (ATC)–links to MS Flight Simulator
▶ Aircraft and Adventure Factory for Microsoft Flight Simulator

M

- ▶ Airport and Facility Directory for Microsoft Flight Simulator
- ▶ Fast Action Paq: The First Challenge–Windows arcade games
- ▶ Flight 685
- ▶ Flight 701
- ▶ Flight Planner for Microsoft Flight Simulator
- ▶ Flight Simulator Pro (FS Pro)–Microsoft Flight Simulator add-on
- ▶ Lhex-I-Con: The Ultimate in Computer Word Strategy Games
- ▶ Lunar Command–manage a lunar colony
- ▶ Quackers line of arcade games for Windows
- ▶ Real Weather Pilot–generate weather for Flight Simulator
- ▶ Rescue Air 911–flight simulator scenarios
- ▶ Scenery upgrades: Grand Canyon, Hawaii, Japan, Tahiti
- ▶ Sound, Graphics, and Aircraft Upgrade for MS Flight Simulator
- ▶ Tower!–air traffic controller tower cab simulator
- ▶ Warpoint–cosmic war in the year 2049

Voice, Standard Support: 214-539-2575 or 800-WEB-FEET

Mansfield Software Group

- ▶ Kedit for DOS and OS/2

Voice, Standard Support: 203-429-8402
Free support for registered users.

Fax Support: 203-487-1185

Online Computer Support

Computer Support via Mansfield's BBS: 203-429-3784

CompuServe: GO PCSVENA

MapLinx Corp.

▶ MapLinx for Windows–mapping package
▶ MapLinx for Windows Professional–mapping package
▶ MapLinx-for-Act–mapping features with Act contact manager

Voice, Standard Support: 214-231-1400 or 800-352-3414

Fax Support: 214-248-2690

Mark of the Unicorn, Inc.

All tech support is free for registered users.

Voice, Standard Support: 617-576-3066
Standard support is available 9 AM to 8 PM, Eastern Time, Monday to Friday.

Fax Support: 617-576-3609
This fax is active 24 hours. Replies are sent as quickly as possible during the voice tech support hours.

Online Computer Support

CompuServe: 71333,3666
Type: GO MOTUSUPPORT in Section 12 in MIDI C Vendor.

Internet: 71333.366@CompuServe.com

Applelink: UNICORN

Internet: unicorn@applelink.apple.com

Masque Publishing

Voice, Standard Support: 303-290-9853

Fax Support: 303-290-6303

Online Computer Support

E-Mail: 71333.1547@CompuServe.com

CompuServe: 71333,1547
Type: GO GAMECPUB

MathSoft, Inc.

- ► CRC Materials Science and Engineering Handbook
- ► Machine Design and Analysis–electronic handbook
- ► MathCAD–mathematical analysis tool and scientific word processor
- ► MathCAD Advanced Math Applications Pack
- ► MathCAD Civil Engineering Applications Pack
- ► MathCAD Electrical Engineering Applications Pack
- ► MathCAD for Windows–math analysis tool and science word processor
- ► MathCAD Numerical Methods Applications Pack
- ► MathCAD Signal Processing Functions Pack
- ► Mathcad Treasury, The–electronic engineering reference handbook
- ► Standard Handbook of Engineering Calculations–CD-ROM
- ► Statistics I: Tests and Estimation
- ► Statistics II: Modeling and Simulation

Voice, Standard Support: 617-577-1778

Fax Support: 617-252-5666

The MathWorks, Inc.

- ► Matlab–science and engineering computation system
- ► Matlab Extended Symbolic Math Toolbox–MATLAB option

The MathWorks, Inc.

- ▶ Matlab for Windows–science and engineering computation system
- ▶ Matlab Frequency Domain System Identification Toolbox
- ▶ Matlab Hi-Spec Toolbox–higher order spectral analysis
- ▶ Matlab Model Predictive Control Toolbox–control system design
- ▶ Matlab Neural Network Toolbox–research and application development
- ▶ Matlab Optimization Toolbox–option to Matlab software
- ▶ Matlab Statistics Toolbox–MATLAB option
- ▶ Matlab Symbolic Math Toolbox–MATLAB option
- ▶ MV-RMAC–image-processing software
- ▶ MV1 and MV2 frame grabber boards
- ▶ Neural Network Toolbox–add-on for Matlab/Simulab
- ▶ Signal Processing Toolbox
- ▶ Simulink–nonlinear dynamic system simulation and analysis
- ▶ Simulink for Windows–system simulation and analysis

Voice, Standard Support: 508-653-1415

Fax Support: 508-653-2997

Telex: 910-240-5521

Online Computer Support

Internet: info@mathworks.com

World Wide Web: Internet WWW: http://mathworks.com

Matrox Graphics, Inc.

- ▶ A/B Roll Matrox Studio–Matrox Studio entry-level version

- ▶ HiPER Plus–graphics accelerator based on S386C924 chip set
- ▶ HiPer VGA–SuperVGA graphics/accelerator board
- ▶ Illuminator 16/AT–real-time frame capture and display controller
- ▶ Illuminator Pro–24 bit video capture board
- ▶ Image-1280 Asynchronous Digitizer (ASD) board
- ▶ Image-1280 Color Digitizer (CLD) board
- ▶ Image-1280 Real-Time Processor (RTP) board
- ▶ iTOOLS–imaging application development software
- ▶ M-Win 1280 VGA graphics board
- ▶ Magnum Series of graphics controllers for ISA bus
- ▶ Matrox Animation Xpress (MAX)–graphics board and JPEG software
- ▶ Matrox Comet–PCI bus color and monochrome frame grabber
- ▶ Matrox Marvel–video-in-a-window and frame capture board
- ▶ Matrox Marvel II–professional PCI bus multimedia controller
- ▶ Matrox MGA Ultima II PCI–64-bit graphics card
- ▶ Matrox MVP–image processing board
- ▶ Matrox NetSwitch/16–16-port Ethernet switch on a PC board
- ▶ Matrox Studio–desktop video suite on five EISA boards
- ▶ Matrox Video Producer–Windows-based video editing software
- ▶ MG-128–1280×1024, 256-color, high-resolution graphics board
- ▶ MG-3D–1024×768 high-resolution graphics board
- ▶ MG-3D Ultra EISA-based 1280×1024 hi-resolution graphics board
- ▶ MGA Impression–high-resolution graphics board with accelerator

Matrox Graphics, Inc.

- ▶ MGA Impression Plus–high-resolution graphics board with accelerator
- ▶ MGA Impression Plus 200–high-resolution graphics board with accelerator
- ▶ MGA Impression-PRO–high-resolution, true-color graphics board
- ▶ MGA Ultima–64-bit graphics accelerator board, PCI/VESA
- ▶ MGA Ultima Plus–64-bit graphics accelerator board
- ▶ MGA Ultima Plus 200–64-bit graphics accelerator board
- ▶ MGA Ultima-VAFC–PCI bus graphics accelerator board
- ▶ MGA Video Pro–video encoder board
- ▶ MP-860 EISA parallel processor board
- ▶ Personal Producer System–video editing system
- ▶ PG Series Graphics Controllers
- ▶ Titania–3D digital video effects board for Matrox Studio
- ▶ Toccata–serial 4:2:2 (D1) standard input/output board
- ▶ VGO-X Series videographics overlay card using C&T 82C452 VGA

Voice, Standard Support: 514-685-0270

Fax Support: 514-685-0174

Online Computer Support

   Computer Support via Matrox BBS: 514-685-6008

McAfee Associates, Inc.

- ▶ Clean-Up–virus remover
- ▶ FILE SHIELD–checks executable files for viruses when run
- ▶ LAN Support Center–Windows help desk application

M

- ▶ McAfee BrightWorks–integrated network management utilities
- ▶ NETSCAN–network version of VIRUSCAN
- ▶ NETShield–antivirus software for NetWare file servers
- ▶ OS/2 Clean–virus remover
- ▶ OS/2 NETSCAN–virus scanner
- ▶ OS/2 SCAN–virus scanner
- ▶ Pro-Scan–antivirus software
- ▶ SENTRY–checks entire system for viruses when booted
- ▶ VCOPY–DOS COPY command replacement with virus protection
- ▶ VIRUSCAN–virus protection and recovery software
- ▶ VSHIELD–memory-resident virus protection program

Our software is sold to businesses on a site-license basis with a subscription model. The subscriptions run for two years and include all bug-fix and feature updates, version upgrades, and unlimited technical support.

Voice, Standard Support: 408-988-3832 or 408-988-4181

Standard support is available 6 AM to 5 PM, Pacific Time, Monday to Friday (excluding major holidays). Technical assistance is free to registered users with a grant number.

Fax Support: 408-970-9727

FAX-on-demand system: 408-988-3034

Online Computer Support

Computer Support via McAfee's BBS: 408-988-4004
Alternate BBS: 408-988-2871
This BBS provides technical support and copies of McAfee's software 24 hours a day (except

McAfee Associates, Inc.

when down for scheduled maintenance). It has 30 lines running at 14.4Kbps, and line settings are 8 data, no parity, 1 stop bit, and flow-control set to hardware or none.

Internet:
E-mail address: support@mcafee.com.
McAfee also has ftp and www servers available, which are mcafee.com and www.mcafee.com, respectively.

America OnLine: Keyword: MCAFEE

CompuServe: 76702,1714
Through the McAfee Virus Help Forum
Type: GO MCAFEE

World Wide Web: webroot@mcafee.com

Media Vision, Inc.

▶ Pro Audio Spectrum 16
▶ Reno
▶ Memphis

Skip McIlvaine of Media Vision, Inc.

Skip McIlvaine is a Product Support Specialist for Media Vision, Inc. He serves as a liaison between Customer Service/Technical Support and the rest of the company, and refers to his job as the "technician to the technicians." His daily activities include advising the engineering, marketing, and other departments about the technical support ramifications of every aspect of each new product.

"We are responsible for making every new product as easy to support as possible," says McIlvaine. "This process usually includes reengineering sound cards, video cards, video-capture cards, CD-ROM drives, installation software, and third-party products." Product Support Specialists thus walk each new product completely through development and production, assuring quality and supportability.

M

- ▶ Pro 3-D soundcard
- ▶ Pro Sonic 16 soundcard
- ▶ Pro Graphics 1024 videocard
- ▶ Pro Audio Spectrum 16 for Macintosh
- ▶ Pro Movie Studio
- ▶ Multimedia kits
- ▶ Thunder & Lightning card

Voice, Standard Support: 800-638-2807, 510-770-9905

Standard support is available Monday through Friday, 6 AM to 8 PM, Pacific Time, and Saturday and Sunday, 8 AM to 4 PM, Pacific Time.

Automated support also is available 24 hours a day, 7 days a week.

Fax Support: 510-770-8648, 510-252-4490

Online Computer Support

Computer support via Media Vision's BBS: 510-770-0527

McIlvaine also tracks problems, incompatibilities, and conflicts with third-party hardware and software, while keeping all involved parties informed. He says this process includes the acquisition of many third-party products, and subsequent testing and trouble-shooting. "I also evaluate all third-party products that are being considered for bundling with our own products," he says. "I do so on a basis of technical merit, supportability, and content."

When asked what he likes best about his job, McIlvaine says, "I believe fun to be at the root of every multimedia company's core business." He says it is Media Vision's objective to bring more fun and make it easier to have fun by popularizing the entertainment and educational aspects of multimedia and doing so for less.

"Many people here have a joystick and speakers on their desk," says McIlvaine. "It's crazy. It's almost

Continued . . .

CompuServe: GO MEDIAVISION

Internet: techsupp@mediavis.com
ww//http:mediavis.com

America OnLine: Type: MEDIAVISION

Online Service:
Phone: 510-252-4521
Fax: 510-623-5742

Worldwide Support

Australia
Phone: 800-621-399
BBS: 035-252-799

France
Phone: 33-1-30-48-07-70
33-1-30-48-08-09

Germany (European headquarters)
Phone: 49-0-2957-79-9629
Fax: 49-0-2957-79-510

like working in an arcade; sounds and music emanate from every cubicle and office."

McIlvaine studied computers throughout high school and college and received degrees in Information Systems, Marketing, and Russian Literature. "Marketing and Russian, I feel, rounded out my education," he says. "But technology was where my heart was. The more complicated the subject matter, the more I became intrigued."

After college, McIlvaine moved to Silicon Valley to pursue a career in multimedia, where he eventually came to Media Vision as a technician. "It is clearly an enjoyable place to work," he says.

McIlvaine recalls the most difficult situation he has faced: "It was when I had to solve a purist's complaint about the incompatible termination of a particular SCSI CD-ROM drive with a third-party host adapter. The discussion over the phone involved jumpers on the CD-

M

New Zealand
   Phone: 0-800-442-249

U.K.
   Phone: 44-264-333-406
   44-264-358-646
   Fax: 44-264-334-443

Megahertz

▶ Modems

Voice, Standard Support: 801-320-7777

Fax Support:
   Automated Faxback system via our 800-LAPTOPS
   (527-8677) phone number as well as our RMA
   (Return Merchandise Authorization) department.

Online Computer Support

   Computer Support via Megahertz BBS: 801-320-8840

   CompuServe: GO MEGAHERTZ

ROM drive, jumpers on the SCSI controller, the creation
of an ASCII.DAT file passing to DEBUG to punch certain
memory addresses, the editing of several system configuration files, and the exchange of two defective (customer-
damaged) parts. The hardest part was the fact that he
spoke French and I didn't."

   The most common problem McIlvaine hears is an
IRQ conflict between a sound card and some other device. He also finds the improper version of MSCDEX
(Microsoft CD-ROM Extensions) causes many problems.

   As for what callers can do to help McIlvaine arrive
at a solution for them, he says that preparation is the
key. "It is always best for the customer to familiarize
themselves with the different components inside their
computer." He says you should know who made the
motherboard, the BIOS, the chipset, the video card,
among other basic features.

Continued . . .

Megatech Software

Voice Standard Support and Hint Line
310-539-9177
Standard support is available 9 AM to 6 PM, Pacific Time, Monday to Friday. Megatech's technical support and hint line is free to registered players. Customers need to mail in their registration card that's included with every game.

Online Computer Support

Computer Support via Megatech's BBS: 310-539-7739
Megatech maintains a 24-hour, 5-node free public BBS where callers can call in with a modem and leave questions to their Sysops or view/download hints. Hint files are password-protected (users need to use the code list in their manual or code wheel to select the correct password). The BBS offers 2400 to 14.4K speeds; the callers modem settings must be set to 8-N-1.

He also suggests that callers be in front of their computer when they call. "Callers often complain of an error message that they have forgotten and haven't written down," he explains. "They are unable to explain the specific problem, cannot perform necessary tests, and cannot successfully implement the fix if not seated at the computer . . .. This is frustrating for both parties involved, and I would advise against calling tech support and expecting that the person on the other end has a magical fix for your specific problem."

As for users who want to educate themselves, McIlvaine says the best way to learn is by experience and experiment. He says that most people cannot learn computers from a book nor a videotape. "The best way is to try something different, strike out on your own, face the consequence of a mistake and try not to fear

M

Internet: 74431,2473@compuserve.com

Compuserve: 74431,2473
Type: GO GAMDPUB and visit section 10, our section in the Game Publishers D+ Forum.

Merit Studios

Voice, Standard Support: 214-385-2957
Standard support is available 10 AM to 5 PM, Central Time, Monday to Friday.

Fax Support: 214-385-8205

Metz Software

▶ METZ Desktop Manager–MS Windows menuing system
▶ METZ Desktop Navigator–MS Windows directory utility
▶ METZ Dialer–pop-up speed dialer using modem

mistakes." He says that over time, simple familiarity and experience will teach you more than any book.

When faced with solving problems on their own, McIlvaine strongly advises users to do one thing: overcome fear. He says this is the single most distracting factor involved in computer literacy. "People become overwhelmed by manuals, README files, online documentation, and give up hope in ever feeling confident in their ability and understanding."

"New users should ask a more confident user to spend time with them on their own machines," says McIlvaine. "A dissertation on the advantages of the computer's Complimentary Metal Oxide Semiconductor is not necessary, but a quick explanation of how the computer does what it does can be a great first step towards a more complete understanding of the cause and effect of future technical problems."

- ▶ METZ File F/X–set of file and application management utilities
- ▶ METZ Freemem–free memory display for MS Windows
- ▶ METZ Lock–security application for MS Windows
- ▶ METZ Phones–auto-dialer and telephone directory for MS Windows
- ▶ METZ Runner–utility for running applications
- ▶ METZ Task Manager–Windows Task List application replacement
- ▶ METZ Time–pop-up date and time display for MS Windows

Voice, Standard Support: 206-641-4525

Fax Support: 206-644-6026

Online Computer Support

    Computer Support via METZ BBS: 206-644-3663

    CompuServe: 75300,1627

    Internet: 75300,1627@CompuServe.com

    America OnLine: METZSoft

Micah Development Corp.

- ▶ Full Armor For Windows–system security software
- ▶ Full Armor–security utility
- ▶ Full Shield PC Protector–nonmemory-resident security utility
- ▶ WindoWasher–performance and disk space optimizer tool

Voice, Standard Support: 617-641-1500 or 800-653-1783

Fax Support: 617-641-1973

M

Micrografx, Inc.

- ▶ ABC Flowcharter–professional flow diagram and charting program
- ▶ ABC SnapGrafx–Windows business charts and graphics software
- ▶ ABC ToolKit–Windows-based process management software
- ▶ Charisma–desktop presentation software
- ▶ Crayola Amazing Art Adventure–electronic painting program
- ▶ Crayola Art Studio–electronic painting program
- ▶ Draw Plus–interactive graphics editor and drawing package
- ▶ Graph Plus–chart/graph creation software
- ▶ Graphics Works for Windows
- ▶ Headline Typefaces IV
- ▶ In-A-Vision–technical illustration and CAD drawing package
- ▶ Instant ORGCharting!
- ▶ Micrografx Clip Art Libraries
- ▶ Micrografx Designer–graphic design software
- ▶ Micrografx Mirrors–Windows to OS/2 PM software development tools
- ▶ PhotoMagic for Microsoft Windows–image manipulation software
- ▶ Picture Publisher–image-editing program
- ▶ Structured Graphics Toolkit–dynamic link libraries
- ▶ Windows Draw–illustration program
- ▶ Windows Graph
- ▶ Windows OrgChart–organization charting software
- ▶ XPort–graphics file translation utility

Voice, Standard Support: 214-994-6476
Support numbers differ according to product:
ABC Flowcharter: 214-234-2694

ABC SnapGrafx: 214-497-6499
Picture Publisher: 214-497-6495
Designer, technical edition: 214-497-6494
Windows Draw: 214-234-2694

Online Computer Support

Computer Support via Micrografx's BBS:
214-644-4194

America OnLine: Keyword: GO MAX

CompuServe: Type: GO MICROGRAFX

Worldwide Support
Japan
Phone: 81353853130

France
Phone: 33169181950

United Kingdom
Phone: 440483747526

Germany
Phone: 089-2603830
Fax: 089-263277

Microleague Interactive Software

Voice, Standard Support: 302-368-9990 ext. 210
Standard support is available 8:30 AM to 4:30 PM,
Eastern Time, Monday to Friday.

Fax Support: 302-368-8600
CompuServe ID–71154,2271

Online Computer Support

CompuServe: Game Publishers D forum

MicroMedium, Inc.

▶ Digital Trainer Professional
▶ 5000+ image library CD
▶ Industrial 1000 image library CD

Voice, Standard Support: 919-558-9225
Support is free for all users of MicroMedium, Inc.
Products. Support is for authoring of industrial
training applications for Windows using the
Digital Trainer Professional series of tools.

Fax Support: 919-558-9338

Online Computer Support

CompuServe: GO MICROMEDIUM

Micronetics Design

Voice, Standard Support: 301-258-2605

Fax Support: 301-840-8943

Online Computer Support

Computer Support via Micronetics BBS: 301-948-6825

E-mail: info@rios.mnetx.com

Worldwide Support
England
Phone: 44-734-890500
Fax: 44-734-891483

Switzerland
Phone: 41-91-593947
Fax: 41-91-594638

Germany
Phone: 49-6102-25356
Fax: 49-6102-25259

MicroProse

▶ Gaming software

Voice, Standard Support: 410-771-1151
Standard support is available 9 AM to 5 PM,
Eastern Time, Monday to Friday.

Fax Support: 410-771-9150

Online Computer Support

    Computer Support via MocroProse BBS: 410-785-1841

    Prodigy: XHFK15D

    America OnLine: MicroProse

    CompuServe: 76004,2223

Microsoft

Support Network Information: 800-936-3500
(United States)
800-668-7975 (Canada)

Voice, Standard Support

    Standard support is available, depending upon
specific products:

    Desktop Applications
Access: 206-635-7050 (U.S.) or 905-568-3503
(Canada)
Excel for Macintosh: 206-635-7080 (U.S.) or
905-568-3503 (Canada)
Excel for Windows and OS/2: 206-635-7070 (U.S.)
or 905-568-3503 (Canada)
Money: 206-635-7131 (U.S.) or 905-568-3503
(Canada)
Multimedia Products: 206-635-7072 (U.S.) or
905-568-3503 (Canada)
Office for the Macintosh: 206-635-7055 (U.S.) or
905-568-3503 (Canada)
Office for Windows: 206-635-7056 (U.S.) or
905-568-3503 (Canada)
Office–Switcher Line: 206-635-7041 (U.S.) or
905-568-3503 (Canada)
PowerPoint: 206-635-7145 (U.S.) or 905-568-3503
(Canada)

![Microsoft logo M]

Profit: 800-723-3333 (U.S.) or 905-568-3503
(Canada)
Project: 206-635-7155 (U.S.) or 905-568-3503
(Canada)
Publisher: 206-635-7140 (U.S.) or 905-568-3503
(Canada)
Schedule+: 206-635-7049 (U.S.) or 905-568-3503
(Canada)
Video for Windows: 206-635-7172 (U.S.) or
905-568-3503 (Canada)
Windows Entertainment Products: 206-637-9308
(U.S.) or 905-568-3503 (Canada)
Word for the Macintosh: 206-635-7200 (U.S.) or
905-568-3503 (Canada)
Word for the MS-DOS: 206-635-7210 (U.S.) or
905-568-3503 (Canada)
Word for Windows: 206-462-9673 (U.S.) or
905-568-3503 (Canada)
Works for the Macintosh: 206-635-7160 (U.S.) or
905-568-3503 (Canada)
Works for MS-DOS: 206-635-7150 (U.S.) or
905-568-3503 (Canada)
Works for Windows: 206-635-7130 (U.S.) or
905-568-3503 (Canada)

Personal operating systems
MS-DOS 6.0 and MS-DOS 6.2 upgrades:
206-646-5104 (U.S.) or 905-568-3503 (Canada)
Windows and Windows for Workgroups:
206-637-7098 (U.S.) or 905-568-3503 (Canada)
Mouse, Microsoft BallPoints, Windows Sound
System, and other Microsoft Hardware:
206-635-7040 (U.S.) or 905-568-3503 (Canada)

Developmental tools
Basic PDS: 206-635-7053 (U.S.) or 905-568-3503
(Canada)

Microsoft

Delta: 206-635-7019 (U.S.) or 905-568-3503
(Canada)
Excel SDK: 206-635-7048 (U.S.) or 905-568-3503
(Canada)
FORTRAN: 206-635-7015 (U.S.) or 905-568-3503
(Canada)
Fox products for MS-DOS and Windows:
206-635-7191 (U.S.) or 905-568-3503 (Canada)
Fox products for the Macintosh: 206-635-7192
(U.S.) or 905-568-3503 (Canada)
Macro Assembler (MASM): 206-646-5109 (U.S.)
or 905-568-3503 (Canada)
Profiler: 206-635-7015 (U.S.) or 905-568-3503
(Canada)
QuickBasic: 206-646-5101 (U.S.) or 905-568-3503
(Canada)
QuickC: 206-635-7010 (U.S.) or 905-568-3503
(Canada)
Test for Windows: 206-635-7052 (U.S.) or
905-568-3503 (Canada)
Visual Basic Professional Toolkit: 206-646-5105
(U.S.) or 905-568-3503 (Canada)
Visual Basic: 206-646-5105 (U.S.) or 905-568-3503
(Canada)
Visual C/C++: 206-635-7007 (U.S.) or
905-568-3503 (Canada)
Windows Software Development Kit:
206-635-3329 (U.S.) or 905-568-3503 (Canada)

Standard support in the United States is
available 6 AM to 6 PM, Pacific Time, Monday
through Friday, excluding holidays. In Canada,
you can call between 8 AM and 8 PM, Eastern
Time, excluding holidays. Support for personal
operating system products and development
tools products is available for 90 days from your
first call to a support engineer.

Microsoft

Automated Support:

Automated phone support is available, depending upon specific categories:

Desktop Applicants FastTips: 800-936-4100
Personal Operating Systems FastTips: 800-936-4200
Development Tools FastTips: 800-936-4300
Advanced Systems FastTips: 800-936-4400

Automated phone support is available 24 hours, 7 days a week in the United States and Canada. You can access technical articles and the answers to the most frequently asked questions via voice mail, fax, and U.S. mail.

Priority Support:

Microsoft's priority support is designed to let you select the support coverage that best suits your product and support needs 24 hours a day, 7 days a week. You can charge calls to your credit card, make calls via a 900 number, or purchase an annual subscription or support 10-pack.

900 Number Support (not available in Canada):
Priority Comprehensive: 900-555-2100
Priority Desktop Applications: 900-555-2000
Priority Development with Desktop: 900-555-2311
Priority Personal Operating Systems: 900-555-2000

Credit Card Support:
Priority Comprehensive: 800-936-5900 (U.S.)
Priority Desktop Applications: 800-936-5700 (U.S.) or 800-668-7975 (Canada)
Priority Development with Desktop: 800-936-5800 (U.S.)
Priority Personal Operating Systems: 800-936-5700 (U.S.) or 800-668-7975 (Canada)

Microsoft

Premier Support:

Microsoft's premier support is designed to provide personalized, comprehensive support for mission-critical, help desk, and development/OEM adaption environments. Premier support includes unlimited telephone and electronic service requests. Support is available 24 hours a day, 7 days a week.

Premier Comprehensive provides unlimited support on all Microsoft products and covers mission-critical projects, inhouse development, and help desk needs. Premier Development provides unlimited support for any development or OEM adaption issues for Microsoft products.

Sales and Information: 800-936-3500 (U.S.) or 800-668-7975 (Canada)

TT/TDD Support: 206-635-4948 (U.S.) or 905-568-9641 (Canada)

Online Computer Support

CompuServe: 800-848-8100, ext. 524 (United States and Canada)

Microsoft Download Service:
This allows access by modem to sample programs, device drivers, patches, software updates, and programming aids. Call 206-936-6735 (United States) or 905-507-3022 (Canada).

OnLine for Windows Support: 800-443-4672

Special Information

Microsoft also offers subscription programs that provide regular and comprehensive technical, strategic, and resource information:

Microsoft

Microsoft TechNet: 800-344-2121 x348 (U.S.) or
800-563-9048 (Canada)

Microsoft Developer Network: 800-759-5474 (U.S.)
or 800-563-9048 (Canada)

Microsoft CD-ROM Installation: 206-635-7033
(U.S.)

Microsoft Certified Professionals: 800-765-7768
(U.S.)

MicroSpeed, Inc.

- ▶ Cursor Deluxe–creative cursors for Windows
- ▶ Fast 88–accelerator card
- ▶ FastTRAP–trackball controller with Trackwheel
  for third axis
- ▶ Keyboard Deluxe–small footprint replacement
  keyboard
- ▶ MicroTRAC–trackball controller
- ▶ Mouse Utilities
- ▶ PC-Trac–trackball controller
- ▶ PDA–bus mouse interface for serial mice
- ▶ PowerTrac–trackball system designed for Windows
- ▶ WinTrac (PD 930) trackball controller

Voice, Standard Support: 510-490-1403 or
  800-232-7888

Fax Support: 510-490-1665

Online Computer Support

Computer Support via MicroSpeed's BBS:
510-490-1664

MIDI Solutions

Voice, Standard Support: 800-561-MIDI (6434)
  Canada: 604-794-3013
  Both of these technical support services are free
  of charge to MIDI Solutions customers.

MIDI Solutions

MountainGate Data Systems

▶ DataShuttle 1000–single 5.25" removable disk drives
▶ DataShuttle 2100–dual 5.25" removable disk drives
▶ DataShuttle 2200–dual 5.25" lockable disk drives
▶ Immunity Disk Mirroring Software for PassPort XL
▶ IncreMeg–127MB to 2.1GB hard disk storage subsystems
▶ IncreMeg 6000–quad drive 12GB hard disk storage subsystem
▶ MaTrix RAID Disk Array
▶ PassPort XL–fully enclosed 3.5" removable hard disk drive
▶ Pathfinder–rugged optical disk drives
▶ VideoGig–1.7 to 4.1 GB 3.5" removable hard disk drives

Voice, Standard Support: 702-851-9393 or 800-556-0222

Fax Support: 702-851-5533

Worldwide Support
France
   Phone: 33142653980
   Fax: 33142653971

Germany
   Phone: 490843147048
   Fax: 490843149925

United Kingdom
   Phone: 440256464767
   Fax: 44025659748

M*USA Business Systems

Voice, Standard Support: 214-490-0100

You can call in on this number and pay $1.50 per minute with a 10-minute minimum.

Fax Support: 214-404-1955

Faxback: 214-980-7200

You can pay $10.00 to have a fax answered for you. Please note that these are payable via Amex, MC, Visa, check, or money order.

You can access this fax on-demand system 24 hours a day, 7 days a week. On this system, you will be able to access predefined faxes in response to commonly asked questions. Please call 214-980-7200 from your fax machine to access this information.

You can call in on the 900-988-6872 number and pay $2.00 per minute.

Priority/Pay-for-service Support

DOS/Mac/Win:

  CashBIZ (30 days free)–1 year: $50

Windows:

  Perfect Time–1 year: $100

DOS:

  Pacioli 2000 2.0 Accounting–1 year: $75

  Pacioli 2000 2.0 Accounting–30 days: $30

  Pacioli Payroll–1 year: $75

  Pacioli Payroll–30 days: $30

  Pacioli Accounting & Payroll–1 year: $125

  Pacioli 2000 3.0 Accounting–1 year: $150

  Perfect Payroll–1 year: $75

  Mondial Accounting(6 months free)–1 year: $150

Also included with the yearly support are free updates. Only shipping and handling of $7.50 is charged.

Music Quest, Inc.

Voice, Standard Support: 214-881-7408

Priority Support: 805-873-2551

This number will ring only when a support agent is available to answer the call immediately. Keep in mind, however, that this number is likely to be busy during periods of highest demand, which occur in the mornings and during lunchtime.

Fax Support: 214-422-7094

Online Computer Support

CompuServe:
Music Quest section in MIDIAVEN
Type: GO MUSICQUEST

CompuServe: 75300,2770

Musicator

Voice, Standard Support: 916-756-9807 or 510-251-2500

All Musicator technical support in the US and Canada is free for registered users.

Online Computer Support

Compuserve: 74431,40
Type: GO MCATOR
Musicator section of the MIDI B Vendor forum

Internet:
E-Mail address: 74431.40@compuserve.com

Worldwide Support

Check the Musicator section of the MIDI B Vendor forum.

M

Mustang Software, Inc.

▶ Wildcat, Qmodem, Olx

Online Computer Support

Computer Support via Mustang's BBS: 805-873-2400
Feel free to look around, download any files on
the system that might be of use to you, or leave
a public message in the appropriate area if you
need a question answered. This method of
obtaining support is especially good if you want
expert guidance regarding the more advanced
features from MSI staff and other callers.

CompuServe: Type: GO PCSVENA, then select
SubTopic 9.

GEnie: Go to the MUSTANG RoundTable with the
command MOVE 680.

America OnLine: Keyword: MUSTANG

Internet: support@mustang.com

MSI SupportNET:
A large number of BBS systems carry the MSI
SupportNET echo conferences throughout the US
and Canada. Support BBSs also can be found in
the United Kingdom, Australia, and Norway.

Worldwide Support
Scandinavia
  PCS Security: +47 2 583358

United Kingdom
  Telesystems: +44 494891903

Australia
  Banksia: +61 2 418 7963

Special Information
If you are unable to find the answer to a
question or if you just need a quick explanation,

please give Mustang a voice call between 9 AM and 5 PM, Pacific Time. You can reach technical support at 805-873-2550.

☎ The fastest way to speak to a tech support specialist is to call the main support number, where your call will be answered by the first available agent.

Nanao USA Corp.

- ▶ FlexScan 6300–21" 1664×1200 monochrome monitor
- ▶ FlexScan 6500–21" 1664×1200 grayscale monitor
- ▶ FlexScan 9060S–14" 820×620 VGA color monitor
- ▶ FlexScan 9070U–16" 1024×768 VGA color monitor
- ▶ FlexScan 9080i–16" 1280×1024 0.28mm dot pitch monitor
- ▶ FlexScan 9400–20" 1280×1024 monitor
- ▶ FlexScan 9500–20" 1280×1024 monitor
- ▶ FlexScan F340iW–15" display designed for Windows applications
- ▶ FlexScan F550i–17" 1024×768, 0.28mm dot color monitor
- ▶ FlexScan F550iw–17" 1024×768, 0.28mm dot color monitor
- ▶ FlexScan F560iW–17" ultra-high-resolution monitor
- ▶ FlexScan F750i–21" 1280×1024, 0.31mm dot color monitor
- ▶ FlexScan F760iW–21" 0.31mm dot 1280×1024 color monitor
- ▶ FlexScan F780iW–21" 0.26mm dot 1600×120 color monitor
- ▶ FlexScan T2*17–17" Trinitron 1600×1200 color monitor
- ▶ FlexScan T2*20–20" Trinitron 1600×1200 color monitor
- ▶ FlexScan T560i–17" Trinitron tube 1280×1024 monitor
- ▶ FlexScan T660i–20" Trinitron tube 1280×1024 monitor

Voice, Standard Support: 310-325-5202 or 800-800-5202

Fax Support: 310-530-1679

NEC Technologies, Inc.

▶ Versa P
▶ MultiSpin 4Xi
▶ SuperScript Color 3000
▶ MultiSync XE17
▶ Ready P60M

Voice, Standard Support: 800-388-8888
Standard support is available 8:30 AM to 8 PM, Eastern Time, Monday through Friday.

Fax Support: 800-366-0476

Online Computer Support

Computer Support via NEC's BBS: 508-635-4706

America OnLine: Keyword NECTECH or NEC

Kevin Shea of NEC Technologies, Inc.

▶ Versa P, MultiSpin 4Xi, SuperScript Color 3000, MultiSync XE17, Ready P60M

As an advanced media technical support representative for NEC Technologies, it is Kevin Shea's primary function to answer customers' phone inquiries concerning CD-ROM units. Shea says these calls involve assisting with the installation procedure, answering presales technical questions, locating and solving conflicts with other systems devices, and determining if the hardware is faulty.

Shea's favorite aspect of his job is the opportunity to keep abreast of the latest technology, as well as being involved in the preliminary problem-solving cycle. As for what he likes least, Shea says, "What makes this job interesting also can make it frustrating. The magnitude of trying to solve every conflict with every vendor's

CompuServe:
Type: GO NECTECH (this acts as a gateway to NEC's BBS).

Interchange:
Go through the Companies Online index and select NEC Technologies.

Microsoft Network:
To be released mid 1995, but NEC will have its own section.

New Freedom

▶ The Workplace Shell Backup Utility for OS/2 2.*x*
▶ IconEase for OS/2 2.*x*

Fax Support: 717-235-0985

Online Computer Support

CompuServe: 75600,237

Internet: 75600.237@COMPUSERVER.COM

equipment sometimes is like trying to assemble a jigsaw puzzle with missing pieces—it just can't be done."

Shea's computer background stems from his early experience of repairing computer equipment at the component level and field service. With 20 years in the industry, he has worked at numerous companies.

The most difficult problems that Shea says he encounters are situations where the cause is not the hardware, but a combination of memory allocation, device drivers, TSRs, and the software application. "These problems can be extremely difficult to troubleshoot and require the most time to deal with," he says.

"Where do I get device drivers?" is the most common question Shea hears. This confusion arises when people are using another company's controller card, and device drivers generally come from the controller manufacturer.

Continued. . .

New-Ware

- ▶ ArcMaster–shareware ARC file compression utility interface
- ▶ FormatMaster–menu-driven formatter for DOS diskettes
- ▶ FormatMaster for Windows–diskette format utility
- ▶ Power Chess–shareware Chess game with tutoring
- ▶ ZipMaster–shareware ZIP file compression utility interface
- ▶ ZipTest–standalone ZIP file testing utility

Voice, Standard Support: 619-455-6225

Online Computer Support

Computer Support via New-Ware's BBS: 619-455-5226

Computer Support on CompuServe: 71535,665

Shea says the best way that callers can help him arrive at a solution for them is to have basic information available when they place a service call. Callers should know the model number of the unit, model of the controller, system software version, type of computer, and a brief yet specific explanation of the problem.

"The first thing a novice computer user should do is read the manual," says Shea. "Many of technical support's answers are given to customers verbatim from the manual. Most manuals also give general overviews and operating procedures for the equipment."

In addition to self-teaching, Shea gives the same advice for self-helping: "Read the manual. Read the manual. And then read it again."

N

Nirvana Systems, Inc.

- ▶ OmniTrader (for Windows)
- ▶ Nirvana Data Collector for Telescan
- ▶ Nirvana Data Collector for Dow Jones
- ▶ The Director Series for MetaStock

Voice, Standard Support: 512-345-2545
Standard support is available 9 AM to 9 PM,
Central Time, Monday to Friday.

Fax Support: 512-345-4225

Online Computer Support

Computer Support via Nirvana's BBS: 512-345-1098
(2,400 baud, 24 hour)
512-345-1563 (14.4 baud, 24 hour)

Internet: 72662.2166@CompuServe.com

CompuServe: 72662,2166
Type: GO PCSVENJ

Nombas

- ▶ CEnvi

Voice, Standard Support: 617-391-6595
Standard support is available 9 AM to 5 PM,
Eastern Time, Monday to Friday. Nombas
provides free technical support for CEnvi for
Windows, DOS, OS/2, and NT.

Online Computer Support

Computer Support via CEnvi's BBS: 617-391-6595
Ext. 444
Use dial string ATDT16173916595,,,,,44444)

Internet: E-mail address: bsn@world.std.com
Internet mailing list: send message "subscribe
cenvi-cmm" to majordomo@world.std.com

Internet ftp support library: anonymous ftp at
ftp.std.com in the /vendors/CEnvi-Cmm
directories.

☎ CompuServe via support library: See CENVI.DIR
in IBMSYS library 3

Novell

▶ NetWare 4.1 UnixWare AppWare
▶ GroupWise 4.1 InForms SoftSolutions
▶ PerfectOffice 3.0
▶ WordPerfect 6.1
▶ Quattro Pro 6.0
▶ Envoy 1.0
▶ WordPerfect MainStreet titles

Voice, Standard Support: 800-638-9273 or 800-451-
5151 (for WordPerfect products)
Standard support is available 6 AM to 6 PM,
Central Time, Monday through Friday.

Fax Support: 800-638-9273 or 800-228-9960
(WordPerfect's InfoShare)

TDD Support: 800-321-3256 or 801-228-9906

Online Computer Support

Computer Support via Novell's BBS:
Windows/DOS: 801-225-4414
Macintosh: 801-226-1605
UNIX: 801-228-9909

CompuServe: Type: GO NETWIRE

Internet: Via CompuServe

World-Wide Web: Novell
URL:http://www.novell.com

Gopher: gopher.novell.com

FTP: Anonymous FTP to ftp.novell.com

Novell

Worldwide Support

Europe
   Phone: +49 211 5632 744
   Fax: +49 211 5632 772

Australia and Asia
   Phone: +61 2 925 3133
   Fax: +61 2 922 2040

Numera

▶ Visual CADD

Voice, Standard Support: 206-292-TECH (8324)
   Technical support is free until August 1995. At
   which time, Numera is planning to move to a
   paid support model.

Fax Support: 206-622-5382

Online Computer Support

   Computer Support via Numera's BBS: 206-233-0371
   Using Wildcat! 4.0

   *CompuServe: Section 16 in the CADD/CAM/CAE
   Vendors forum*
   Type: GO CADDVEN or GO NUMERA

Special Information

   As Visual CADD is an open architecture CAD
   program, we encourage third-party
   development. With the release of our Developer's
   Kit this fall, we also will institute a separate
   technical support phone group for developers.

Object Design, Inc.

Voice, Standard Support: 617-674-5040

Fax Support: 617-674-5246

Online Computer Support

CompuServe: Type: GO ODIFORUM

Internet: support@odi.com
or support@odi.com for our UNIX users

Special Information

Users are deemed one year of support from the date of the product purchase. Maintenance contracts are needed after this period and are negotiated with the appropriate ObjectStore sales representative.

Objects, Inc.

Voice, Standard Support: 508-777-2800 or
800-424-6644
Standard support is available 9 AM to 6 PM, Eastern Time, Monday to Friday.

Fax Support: 508-777-0180

Online Computer Support

CompuServe: 72662,462

Internet: Info@ObjectsInc.com

Worldwide Support

Hong Kong
Phone: 852-868-6006
Fax: 852-868-9721
CompuServe ID: 100267,3050
Serving: Asia (People's Republic of China, Hong Kong, Taiwan, Singapore, Thailand, Malaysia, Burma, Philippines, Laos, Indonesia, Vietnam, and Cambodia)

Australia
   via Coolgardie Business Services
   Phone: 61-7-855-2333
   Fax: 61-7-855-2364
   CompuServe ID: 100241,435
   Serving: Australia and New Zealand

India
   via Leviathan Systems Pvt. Ltd
   Phone: 91-22-838-9582
   Fax: 91-22-834-2771
   CompuServe ID: 74131,1034
   Serving: India

Italy
   via Forcast Softwarehouse S.R.L.
   Phone: 39-864-210-691
   Fax: 39-864-210-689
   CompuServe ID: 100407,3413
   Serving: Italy

Brazil
   via Generic Hardware/Software, Ltda.
   Phone: 55-11-65-4588
   Fax: 55-11-62-9415
   CompuServe ID: 74454,754
   Serving: Brazil

South Africa
   via ERA International
   Phone: 27-11-789-7669
   Fax: 27-11-886-3373
   CompuServe ID: 100100,415
   Serving: Southern Africa (South Africa,
   Zimbabwe, Botswana, Madagascar,
   Mozambique, Reunion, Mauritius, Zaire, and
   Namibia)

Objects, Inc.

Colombia
  via Chispas Software, Ltda.
  Phone: 57-5-663-1072
  Fax: 57-5-663-1072
  CompuServe ID: 74551,735
  Serving: South America (Colombia, Bolivia,
  Venezuela, Ecuador, Argentina, Chile, and Peru)

Netherlands
  via Covin Zwolle BV
  Phone: 31-38-231120
  Fax: 31-38-212902
  CompuServe ID: 100333,3421
  Serving: The Netherlands

England
  Phone: 0272-728223
  Fax: 0272-770214
  CompuServe ID: 100043,3715
  Serving: The United Kingdom

Odyssey Computing, Inc.

► On-Schedule for Windows–personal information
  manager
► Recipes for Windows–cookbook and food
  manager

Voice, Standard Support: 619-929-7828 or
  800-446-3977

Fax Support: 619-929-1012

Okna Corp.

► DeskTop Set Professional version 4.1
► Address Book for Windows–DeskTop Set without
  calendar
► DeskTop Set–professional organizer for Windows

Voice, Standard Support: 201-909-8600 or
   800-438-6562

Fax Support: 201-909-0688

Online Computer Support

   CompuServe: 71333,2161
   Type: Go OKNA

Special Information

   All technical support questions are answered
   within 24 hours.

Open Windows

▶ PRO UpD8R–Windows file synchronization utility
▶ WinFlash–shareware educational flashcards
   program
▶ WinUpD8R–shareware Windows file
   synchronization utility

Voice, Standard Support: 719-531-0403 or
   800-531-0403

Fax Support: 719-531-0403

Online Computer Support

   CompuServe: 75236,3243

Omnitrend

Voice, Standard Support: 203-678-7679
   Standard support is available 9 AM to 5 PM,
   Eastern Time, Monday to Friday.

Online Computer Support

   Internet: 72662.455@COMPUSERVE.COM

   CompuServe: 72662,455

   GEnie: OMNITREND

Oracle Corp.

Voice, Standard Support: 415-506-1500
Fax Support: 415-506-7200

Origin

- ▶ Wing Commander Armada–multiplayer game
- ▶ System Shock–cyberpunk first person 3D game
- ▶ Ultima 8–another in the Ultima series of games
- ▶ Wing Commander III–single-player Wing Commander game
- ▶ Wings of Glory–World War I flight simulator
- ▶ Bioforge–first in the line of interactive movie adventures

Voice, Standard Support: 512-335-0440
Standard support is available 9 AM to 5 PM, Central Time, Monday to Friday.

Fax Support: 512-331-8559

Online Computer Support

Computer Support via Origin's BBS: 512-331-4446

OSC

- ▶ DECK II–digital audio workstation software
- ▶ Metro–MIDI sequencing software
- ▶ Trans*Port–DAW conversion and track sheet software
- ▶ Poke in the Ear with a Sharp Stick Vols. I, II, and III–CD-ROM sample libraries
- ▶ Textural Ambience–CD-ROM sample library

Voice, Standard Support: 617-969-0754
Standard support is available 8 AM to 4 PM, Pacific Time, Monday to Friday.

Fax Support: 617-928-0038

Online Computer Support

CompuServe: 72662.262
OSC Forum in MIDI C Vendor Forum
Type: GO MIDI

OsoSoft

Voice, Standard Support: 805-526-1759
Standard support is available 7 AM to 4 PM,
Pacific Time, Monday to Friday. OsoSoft offers
free, unlimited support to paid, registered users of
its products. Unregistered users of shareware
versions of OsoSoft products receive only
installation support for the shareware versions
unless they register at the time of the support
call.

Fax Support: 805-528-3074

Online Computer Support

Computer Support via OsoSoft's BBS: 805-528-3753

CompuServe: Type: GO OSOSOFT

Pacific Data Products

Voice, Standard Support: 619-587-4690
Standard support is available 7 AM to 4:30 PM,
Pacific Time, Monday to Friday.

Online Computer Support

Computer Support via Pacific Data's BBS: 619-452-6329

CompuServe: Type: GO PACDATA
PCVEND forum section 14.

Internet: Anonymous ftp site at pacdata.com
where we provide file support.

Packard Bell

Voice, Standard Support for Hardware: 800-733-4411
Standard support is available 24 hours/7 days.
Nonpeak hours are 1 AM to 7 AM, Central Time.

Fax Support for Hardware: 801-579-0092

Voice, Standard Support for Software: 801-579-0161
Standard support is available 6 AM to 6 PM,
Central Time, 7 days a week.

Fax Support for Software: 801-579-0092

Online Computer Support

Computer Support via Packard Bell's BBS: 801-250-1600

☎ Packard Bell Pre-Sales will provide new product
information as well as upgrade information.

Painless Accounting

▶ Painless Accounting–integrated shareware accounting package
▶ Painless Accounting for Windows–shareware accounting package
▶ Painless Accounting/Payroll Companion
▶ Painless Event Processor–shareware event scheduler
▶ Painless Menu Manager–menuing system for hard disks
▶ Painless Payroll
▶ Painless Payroll for Windows–shareware payroll package

Voice, Standard Support: 214-521-9905 or 800-521-9905

Fax Support: 214-596-9164

Online Computer Support

Computer Support via Painless Accounting's BBS: 214-881-0313

CompuServe: 70337,3337

GEnie: K.PIERCE7

Paltex International

▶ EDDi Pro Desktop Video Editing for Windows–uses COM port
▶ EDDi Vision Series Video Editor (Windows) with video overlay board

Voice, Standard Support: 714-838-8833 or 800-321-3334

Fax Support: 714-838-9619

PapPYR

▶ paPYrus
Pay-per-use services for OS/2

Online Computer Support

CompuServe: 71732,3361
OS2SHARE forum

Internet: 71732.3361@CompuServe.com
The product supports the self-publishing, by any
OS/2 user, of pay-per-use books and software.

Papyrus Design Group, Inc.

▶ NASCAR Racing
▶ IndyCar Racing
▶ Indianapolis Motor Speedway
▶ IndyCar Circuits

Voice, Standard Support: 617-868-3103

Standard support is available 9 AM to 5 PM,
Eastern Time, Monday to Friday.

We offer telephone support free of charge. Our
BBS is available 24 hours a day and contains the
latest updates as well as settings and hints from
other drivers. It serves as a great way to find
modem partners in any specific area. Questions
to technical support on any of the online
services will be answered Monday through
Friday during normal business hours.

Fax Support: 617-349-3999

Online Computer Support

Computer Support via Papyrus' BBS: 617-576-7472

America OnLine: Papyrus2 (ID)
Keyword: PAPYRUS

Internet: papyrus@world.std.com

ftp: ftp.std.com
/ftp/vendors/papyrus

CompuServe: 72662,2150
Type: GO PAPYRUS

PC-Kwik Corp.

▶ PC-Kwik Power Disk–disk defragmenter and utility
▶ PC-Kwik Power Pak–system speed-up utility
▶ Super PC-Kwik Disk Accelerator–disk caching utility
▶ Toolbox–Windows Program Manager enhancement/replacement
▶ WinMaster–Windows performance enhancement software

Voice, Standard Support: 503-644-5644 or 800-288-5945

Standard support is available 8 AM to 5 PM, Pacific Time, Monday to Friday. PCS-Kwik also has a Kwik-Service plan whereby, for a price, they will provide an 800 number for technical support.

Fax Support: 503-646-8267

PCSX

Voice, Standard Support: 619-259-9797

Fax Support: 619-481-6474

Online Computer Support

Computer Support via PCSX's BBS: 619-481-6479

CompuServe: 70216,174
OS2BVEN section 2

Internet: support@PCsx.com

Peachtree Software, Inc.

▶ Crystal Accounting–comprehensive Windows accounting software
▶ Double Bonus Bundle–Peachtree Complete II and Data Query II
▶ PeachPay–standalone payroll module
▶ Peachtree Accounting for Macintosh
▶ Peachtree Accounting for Windows
▶ Peachtree Accounting for Windows CD-ROM Edition
▶ Peachtree Basic Accounting
▶ Peachtree Client Write-Up
▶ Peachtree Complete Accounting for DOS
▶ Peachtree Complete II Business Accounting System
▶ Peachtree Complete Network Accounting
▶ Peachtree Data Query III (PDQ III)–custom management reporting
▶ Peachtree Point of Sale

Voice, Standard Support:

Standard support is available 8:30 AM to 5:30 PM, Eastern Time, Monday to Friday. Peachtree offers free installation help by voice. Support contracts and pay per call are available:
For Peachtree Accounting for windows: 404-279-2099
For Peachtree Complete Acct for DOS : 404-923-4318

Fax Support: 404-564-8080 or 404-925-2777

Online Computer Support

Computer Support via Peachtree's BBS: 404-564-8071

CompuServe:
Type: GO PEACHTREE for DOS support (section 10 of the PCsvend F+ forum). Type: GO

WINPEACH (section 10 of the windows 3rd party D forum).

America OnLine: Keyword PEACHTREE

Prodigy: Jump to COMPUTER SOFTWARE

Special Information
Peachtree has a number of support centers available as well. Call 800-626-0941 24 hours 7 days a week for the closest support center near you.

PED Software Corp.

Voice, Standard Support: 408-253-3376

Fax Support: 408-253-1062
Please indicate to "Technical Support Department" on the cover page.

Online Computer Support

CompuServe:
We have PED Software forum under Windows Third Party E Forum.

Prodigy:
Jump to "Member Exchange" and choose Journlist for topic.

Performance Technology, Inc.

Voice, Standard Support: 210-979-2010

Fax Support: 210-979-2011

Online Computer Support

Computer Support via Performance's BBS: 210-979-2012

CompuServe: Type: GO PERFTECH, section 13

Internet: support@perftech.com

Performance Technology, Inc.

Persoft, Inc.

- ▶ Intersect Local Bridge
- ▶ Intersect Remote Bridge
- ▶ IZE–textbase
- ▶ IZE Reader
- ▶ Referee–TSR manager
- ▶ SmarTerm 125–emulates DEC VT125/100/102/52 terminals
- ▶ SmarTerm 220–emulates DEC VT220/100/102/52 terminals
- ▶ SmarTerm 2392–emulates HP 2392 text terminal
- ▶ SmarTerm 240–emulates DEC VT100/220/240/241
- ▶ SmarTerm 320–emulates DEC VT52/100/220/320 terminals
- ▶ SmarTerm 340–emulates DEC VT340 graphics terminal
- ▶ SmarTerm 340 for Windows–VT terminal emulation software
- ▶ SmarTerm 400–emulates DG Dasher 100/200/400 terminals
- ▶ SmarTerm 4014–emulates Tektronix 4014 graphics terminal
- ▶ SmarTerm 420 for Windows–VT terminal emulation software
- ▶ SmarTerm 470–emulates DG D470 and D460/61/50 terminals
- ▶ SmarTerm 470 for Windows–Data General terminal emulation
- ▶ SmartMOVE–communications software

Voice, Standard Support: 608-273-4357

Fax Support: 608-273-8227

Worldwide Support
Germany

Phone:0893616310
Fax: 0893617094

Netherlands
Phone: 310250322100
Fax: 312050222340

Online Computer Support

Computer Support via PerSoft's BBS: 608-273-6595

Phase3 Software Inc.

Voice, Standard Support: 805-641-0775
Phase3 provides 90 days of free phone support
and unlimited free support via BBS, fax, Internet
and CompuServe. Additional voice support after
the initial 90 days can be purchased through
various option plans.

Fax Support: 805-641-0332
QuikTech FAX: 805-641-0684
This fax is used for installation and
configuration questions and other simplistic
technical support.

Online Computer Support

Computer Support via Phase3's BBS: 805-641-3273

CompuServe: 74431,1027
Type: GO PHASE3

Internet FTP: ftp://pacrain.com/pub/phase3

Internet Mail: phase3@pacrain.com

PKWARE, Inc.

- ▶ PK Safe ANSI
- ▶ PKlite–executable file compressor
- ▶ PKlite Professional–executable file compressor
- ▶ PKWARE Data Compression Library–library for
  software developers

PKWARE, Inc.

- ▶ PKWARE Data Compression Library for OS/2
- ▶ PKWARE Data Compression Library for Windows
- ▶ PKzfind/PKZoom File Finder Plus–shareware utility
- ▶ PKzip, PKunzip, PKsfx–shareware file compression
- ▶ PKzmenu–standalone menu-driven version of PKunzip
- ▶ StupenDOS–DOS shell
- ▶ Zipper–PKZIP like utility for MS Windows

Voice, Standard Support: 414-354-8699
Standard support is available 9 AM to 5 PM, Central Time, Monday to Friday.

Fax Support: 414-354-8559

Online Computer Support

Computer Support via PKWARE's BBS: 414-354-8670

CompuServe: 75300,730
Type: GO PKWARE

Internet: PKWARE.Inc@mixcom.com

Power Up Software Corp.

- ▶ Address Book Plus–personal address management
- ▶ Business Plan–guide for creating business plans
- ▶ Calendar Creator Plus–create professional calendars
- ▶ Calendar Creator Plus for Windows–create professional calendars
- ▶ Company Ladder–organization charts
- ▶ DeskMate Form Finisher
- ▶ DOS Director–user interface
- ▶ Express Art/300: Business I and II–clipart for Express Publisher

- ▶ Express Art/300: Education–clipart for Express Publisher
- ▶ Express Art/300: Special Occasions–Express Publisher clipart
- ▶ Express Fonts: Classic–Palacio and Triumvirate Condensed
- ▶ Express Fonts: Flair–Park Avenue & Brush fonts
- ▶ Express Fonts: Stylist–Century Schoolbook and Omega fonts
- ▶ Express Presenter–presentation graphics software
- ▶ Express Publisher–low-end desktop publisher
- ▶ File & Find–organize files, documents, and collections
- ▶ Form Finisher–forms software
- ▶ FormsFile–forms software
- ▶ FormWorx for DOS–graphical forms processing software
- ▶ FormWorx for Windows–graphical forms processing software
- ▶ Labels Unlimited–label maker software
- ▶ Labels Unlimited for Windows–label maker software
- ▶ Letters On-Line–800+ sample documents
- ▶ Name Tag Kit–create professional looking name tags
- ▶ Name That Disk–produce diskette labels
- ▶ Personnel Policy–create company policy manual
- ▶ PowerRunner Pack
- ▶ Present It–business presentations
- ▶ Program Director–menu shell for software applications
- ▶ Quick Schedule Plus–project management software
- ▶ TextAppeal for Windows–text effects for desktop publisher
- ▶ Top Priority–time and task manager

Power Up Software Corp.

- ▶ Typewriter, The–simple electronic typewriter
- ▶ Word Guide–templates for Form Finisher
- ▶ Working Hours–staff scheduling, various formats

Voice, Standard Support: 415-345-0551

Fax Support: 415-345-3793

Practical Peripherals, Inc.

- ▶ Modems

Voice, Standard Support: 805-496-7707 or 805-497-4777

Standard support is available 6 AM to 11 PM, Pacific Time, Monday to Friday, and 8 AM to 5 PM, Pacific Time, Saturday and Sunday.

Fax Support: 805-374-7200
PractiFAX Service: 800-225-4774

Online Computer Support

Computer Support via Practical Peripherals' BBS: 805-496-4445

America Online: jump work PPI

Prodigy: COMPUTER BB

CompuServe: GO PPIFORUM

Internet: COMP.DCOM.MODEMS section

Special Information

You can expect to see a response to any question that is posted on CompuServe on the PPIFORUM within 24 hours. It is more accurately within 10 hours on weekdays and within 24 hours on weekends.

If you would like printed material and have a fax at your disposal, feel free to call the Practical Peripherals PractiFAX (call voice first and you will be prompted for your fax number). The PractiFax can be reached at 800-225-4774.

Primavera Systems, Inc.

- ▶ P3 for Windows–high-end project management/scheduling software
- ▶ P3 for DOS–high-end project management/scheduling software
- ▶ Parade–cost control and performance measurement Software
- ▶ Risk analysis and simulation software
- ▶ SureTrak for DOS
- ▶ SureTrak for Windows
- ▶ Expedition–contract and control software package

Voice, Standard Support:

P3 for Windows, P3 for DOS, Parade, and risk analysis and simulation software: 610-668-3030
SureTrak for DOS and SureTrak for Windows: 801-973-1330
Expedition: 603-284-7272

Fax Support:

P3 for Windows, P3 for DOS, Parade, and risk analysis and simulation software: 610-667-0652
SureTrak for DOS and SureTrak for Windows: 801-973-0953
Expedition: 603-284-6559

Online Computer Support

Computer Support via Primavera's BBS:
P3 for Windows, P3 for DOS, Parade, and risk analysis and simulation software: 610-660-5833
SureTrak for DOS and SureTrak for Windows: 801-973-1073
Expedition: 603-284-6214

CompuServe:
P3 for Windows, P3 for DOS, Parade, and risk analysis and simulation software: 76004,2245

SureTrak for DOS and SureTrak for Windows:
76004,2245
Expedition: 76004,2245

Internet:
P3 for Windows, P3 for DOS, Parade, and risk
analysis and simulation software:
tsupport@primavera.com
SureTrak for DOS and SureTrak for Windows:
ssupport@primavera.com
Expedition: essupport@primavera.com

Worldwide Support
England
   Voice, Standard Support: 011-44-81-748-7300
   This phone number supports all Primavera
   products.
   Fax Support: 011-44-81-748-2846
   CompuServe: 76004,2245
   Internet: uktech@primavera.com

ProCom Technology, Inc.

▶ Storage equipment for PCs and file server
   environments (i.e., Novell, Lan Manager)
▶ CD Towers for networks with 2 to 42 drivers per
   box configuration

Voice, Standard Support: 714-852-1000
   Standard support is available 7:30 AM to 4:30
   PM, Pacific Time, Monday to Friday.

Online Computer Support

   Computer Support via ProCom's BBS: 714-852-1205
   CompuServe: 75300,2312

ProOffice

▶ Personal Addressbook/2 Light
▶ Personal Addressbook/2 for DB2/2
▶ Personal Addressbook/2 Advanced for DB2/2

Fax Support: +49-0-22-08-7-26-25

Online Computer Support

CompuServe:
OS2AVEN Section 1 (Other Vendors)
OS2UGER Section 7 (dt. OS/2 Anwendungen)

CompuServe:
Joerg Janus: 100064,436
Harald Wilhelm: 100031,1250

Internet:
Joerg Janus: 100064.436@CompuServe.com
Harald Wilhelm:
100031.1250@CompuServe.com

ProSoft Corp.

▶ CD Tracker
▶ CD Entry
▶ CD Admin
▶ Carpe Diem for DOS and Windows

Voice, Standard Support: 800-477-6763 or 214-386-0785

Standard support is available 8:30 AM to 5:30 PM, Central Time, Monday to Friday. Extensive support is on a very personable basis and is free as long as the client is using a current version of ProSoft's software.

Online Computer Support

CompuServe: 74431,1120
Keyword: GO CARPEDIEM

PushButton Software

▶ PushButton WORKS–includes a word processor, spreadsheet, database, chart maker, and report writer
▶ PushButton PUBLISH–easy-to-use page layout tool
▶ PushButton DESIGN–drawing tool
▶ PushButton WORD–feature-rich word processor

Voice, Standard Support: 508-485-1683

Standard support is 10 AM to 5 PM, Eastern Time, Monday to Friday. For quicker service when calling, the user should have his/her computer on with the PushButton program up and running. The user also should be ready to provide his/her name and registration number.

Fax Support via Fax Back Program: 508-485-2131

When faxing the technical issue to PushButton, the user should indicate the problem along with any hardware information (i.e., processor type and speed). The user also should provide his/her name, address, and registration number along with a return fax and phone number. After receiving the fax, PushButton will fax back information pertaining to the technical issue.

Online Computer Support

CompuServe: 72662,2566

The user should follow the same procedures as described under the fax back program. After receiving the CompuServe message, PushButton will either reply via CompuServe or send information via fax.

Q

Quantum

▶ Hard disk storage

Voice, Standard Support: 908-788-2799

Online Computer Support

   Computer Support via Quantum's BBS: 408-894-3214

   CompuServe: 75300,3232

   GEnie: QQP

   Delphi: QQP

Quarterdeck

Voice, Standard Support: 310-392-9701
   Standard support is available 7:30 AM to 4:30
   PM, Pacific Time, Monday through Thursday; 10
   AM to 4:30 PM, Friday; 2 AM to 7:30 AM, Extended
   Support Hours. (Extended Hours Support is
   provided by Quarterdeck's support staff in
   Ireland at no additional cost to calling party.)

Automated Voice Support: 800-762-6832

Fax Support: 310-314-3214 or 310-314-3217

Online Computer Support

   Computer Support via Quarterdeck's BBS:
   310-314-3227

   Anonymous FTP site:
   Host name: qdeck.com [149.17.8.10]
   Login: anonymous
   Password: type your E-mail address here
   Notes: Get the README file from ~ /pub for file
   availability

   BIX: Type: JOIN DESQVIEW

   CompuServe: Type: GO QUARTERDECK

Fidonet:
Quarterdeck supports the Fidonet DESQVIEW echo.

Internet:
Type: comp.os.msdos.desqview or support@qdeck.com

MCI Mail: Type: QUARTERDECK

SmartNet: Type: DESQview Conference

Quercus Systems

▶ Rexxterm
▶ Personal Rexx
▶ Rexxlib

Voice, Standard Support: 408-867-7399

Fax Support: 408-867-7489

Online Computer Support

Computer Support via Quercus BBS: 408-867-7488

CompuServe: Type: GO QUERCUS

CompuServe: 75300,2450

Internet: 75300.2450@CompuServe.com

Quorum Software

Voice, Standard Support: 214-789-2939

Fax Support: 214-789-2938

QVoice, Inc.

▶ VoiceLock–Windows-based voice-activated security program

Voice, Standard Support: 201-786-6878

Fax Support: 201-786-5868

Raindrop Software

Fax Support: 214-234-2674

We provide phone support at various fees depending on the product and customer requirements.

Online Computer Support

CompuServe: Type: GO RAINDROP

Special Information

It is important to note that Raindrop operates largely as an engineering firm providing professional Windows software design and development services to specifications. Each of these contracts provide tailored support as required.

Reality OnLine, Inc.

- ▶ Network 2.0 (previously called Smart Investor)
- ▶ Reuters Money
- ▶ Reuters Money Network for Windows 2.0
- ▶ WealthBuilder 3.0 (Mac)
- ▶ WealthBuilder 3.12
- ▶ WealthBuilder for Windows 4.0.

Voice, Standard Support:

For installation support only: 800-777-7424

For continuous support on other matters: 610-239-0720

Standard support is available 8:30 AM to 11:30 PM, Eastern Time, Monday to Friday, except for Wednesday when they are open from 10 AM to 11:30 PM, Eastern Time. Support also is available on Saturday from 9:30 AM to 5 PM, Eastern Time.

Online Computer Support

CompuServe: Type: GO REALITY

Special Information

Reality OnLine has an automated electronic response service, where users can have their technical questions answered immediately 24 hours a day, seven days a week. Users also can contact us through an E-mail facility that is built into each of our programs.

Relay Technology, Inc.

▶ Relay Gateway–asynchronous gateway software
▶ Relay/3270–asynchronous 3270 emulation software
▶ Relay/OpenPort–move data between relational databases
▶ Relay/PC for Windows–communications package
▶ Relay/PC Gold–3270 emulation/mainframe communications software
▶ Relay/PC Gold for Windows–communications software
▶ Relay/PC Gold LAN–communications software
▶ Relay/Transfer–file-transfer utility

Voice, Standard Support: 703-506-0500 or 800-795-8674

Fax Support: 703-506-0510

Rhode Island Soft Systems, Inc.

▶ WinPak–screen savers, fonts, and icons for Windows
▶ RISS Icon Pak–2001 icons plus an icon viewer/changer utility

Voice, Standard Support: 401-767-3106

Fax Support: 401-767-3108

Online Computer Support

Computer Support via RISS BBS: 401-767-3931

CompuServe: Type: GO RISS, Section/Lib 5

Ridax

▶ PM2You–OS/2 remote access facility

Voice, Standard Support: +46 31 196074 or +46 10 6673880
Technical support is free of charge to customers that have bought the commercial versions of our products.

Fax Support: +46 31 196417
With the FAX2You Fax receive option, you can use a fax/modem and receive faxes when PM2You is in host mode.

Online Computer Support

Computer Support via Ridax's BBS: +46 31 196406
Modem speeds: 300 to 28,800 bps

CompuServe: 100114,3127

Internet: d9mikael@dtek.chalmers.se

RoadRunner Computing

Voice, Standard Support: 504-928-0780

Fax Support: 504-928-0802

Online Computer Support

CompuServe: 76436,2426

RPF Software

Fax Support: 404-250-0282

Online Computer Support

CompuServe: 71660,535

OS2SHARE Forum, Section One-OS/2 Shareware
Library One. RPF Zip Control 2.1.2 is there as
ZIPCSTL.ZIP.

Internet: 71660.535@CompuServe.com

Rupp Technology Corp.

- ▶ FastLynx–DOS-based file transfer program
- ▶ WinLynx–Windows/DOS-based file transfer
  program
- ▶ RuppLynx–Windows Wizard Link for 8000/YO-
  6x0/9000 series Wizards
- ▶ Time/Xpense–Wizard application for 9000 series
  Wizard
- ▶ Games Card–Wizard Games for 9000 series
  Wizard

Voice, Standard Support: 602-224-0897

Priority Support: 900-370-2024
  This phone call is $2 per minute.

Fax Support: 602-224-0898
  Faxback: 602-224-0374

Online Computer Support

  CompuServe: 75300,1232
  Forum: Go RUPP (Rupp Technology Folder under
  PCS Vendor C forum)
  We also monitor the Sharp folder (GO Palmtop).

  erica OnLine: Keyword: RuppTech
  Forum: We monitor the Wizard folders (keyword
  PDA).

  Internet: sglasgow@rupp.com

  Newgroups: comp.sys.palmtops
  comp.sys.handhelds comp.sys.pen

  WWW: http://www.rupp.com

  Gopher: gopher.rupp.com

SAW (Software Audio Workshop)

▶ Innovative quality software

Voice, Standard Support: 702-435-9077
  SAW does updates of their products monthly on
  their BBS. SAW also provides free technical
  support.

Fax Support: 702-435-9106

Online Computer Support

  Computer Support via SAW's BBS: 702-435-7186

  CompuServe: Midivendor C or GO SAWSUPPPORT

Scitor Corp.

▶ Project Scheduler 6 for Windows

Voice, Standard Support: 415-570-7700
  Standard support is available 8 AM to 5 PM,
  Pacific Time, Monday to Friday.

Fax Support: 415-570-7807

Online Computer Support

  CompuServe: 72662,261

Sealevel Systems

▶ Communications hardware

Voice, Standard Support: 803-843-4343
  Standard support is available 8 AM to 5 PM,
  Eastern Time, Monday to Friday.

Fax Support: 803-843-3067

Online Computer Support

  CompuServe: Type: GO SEALEVEL or GO PCSVENI

  Internet: tech_support@sealevel.com

Special Information

Sealevel Systems also supports a Developer Assistance Program that is free. This program provides developers and system integrators with additional technical documents and support that aid in developing custom communications applications.

SemWare

▶ The SemWare Editor (TSE)
▶ QEdit DOS Editor
▶ QEdit Advanced
▶ QEdit TSR
▶ QEdit for OS/2

Voice, Standard Support: 404-641-9002

Standard support is available 9 AM to 5 PM, Eastern Time, Monday to Friday. We provide free technical support to our customers for as long as they own the product.

Fax Support: 404-640-6213

Online Computer Support

Computer Support via SemWare's BBS: 404-641-8968

CompuServe: 75300,2710
Type: GO SEMWARE or GO PCSVENE (section 6)

Internet: tech.support@semware.atl.ga.us

Local BBS:
SemWare conferences on the FidoNet, Global-Link, ILink, Intelec, MetroLink, PlanoNet, RelayNet (RIME), SmartNet, U'NI-net, and W-Net mail networks.

Shapeware Corp.

Voice, Standard Support: 206-521-4600

Standard support is available 6 AM to 5 PM, Pacific Time, Monday to Friday. We offer 90 days of free technical support based on the first call date. Upgrades come with 30 days of free support. After that we have a year support contract for $45, $35 for 6 months, or $12 per call.

Fax Support: 206-521-4600

Fax Information System: 206-521-4550

Online Computer Support

Internet: tsdirect@shapeware.com

CompuServe: 71333,1567
Type: GO VISIO

Special Information

Shapeware also has a developer support program that is for people with programming questions. The cost for that is $200 for 6 months or $35 per call. When customers purchase developer support, they receive access to a special phone line, fax line, and Internet address. Shapeware's open phone hours for developer support are currently 8 AM to 12 PM, Pacific Time.

ShowCase Corp.

Voice, Standard Support: 507-288-5922

Standard support is available 8 AM to 5 PM, Central Time, Monday to Friday, excluding holidays. Technical support services are available to all customers that are paying for annual maintenance as confirmed in the

licensing agreement. Telephone support is
unlimited for usage, installation, and
configuration questions.

Online Computer Support

CompuServe: Type: GO SHOWCASE
Technical bulletins are also provided on
CompuServe.

Special Information

ShowCase technical support attempts to provide
an answer during the first call. If this is not
possible, customers will be asked to provide
further information that can be sent by mail,
fax, telephone, or CompuServe. Support then
will continue with the problem analysis when
the information arrives. When there is limited
availability of support technicians due to high
call volumes, customers will be given the option
to leave a message. ShowCase technical support
will respond within four hours of the initial
contact. Call escalation will be handled through
the technical support manager.

Online Call Tracking
ShowCase maintains an online call tracking
system–a database of customers, locations,
contacts, problem, and product details. Support
technicians access this database directly and
enter in the customer information. To expedite
the call, customers should be prepared to
provide their company name, contact name,
and telephone number. When calling the first
time to Support, this process might take longer
to gather the details prior to dealing with your
problem. Support will appreciate the
cooperation for our mutual benefit.

Nonmaintenance Customers

Customers not buying maintenance can receive technical support through an hourly contract with the support organization. Once the signed agreement is received, Support will assist the customer with any usage or configuration questions. If a problem is identified as a code defect, all charges will be waived.

Worldwide Support

☎ International support will be handled in a similar approach through the ShowCase Europe technical support team.

Voice, Standard Support: 45-98-79-15-15

Fax Support: 45-98-79-14-14

☎ The ShowCase Corp. Services Office provides ShowCase software training and consulting services.

Voice, Standard Support: 708-384-5600

Fax Support: 708-384-5623

Sierra On-Line

Voice, Standard Support: 206-644-4343
Standard support is available 8:15 AM to 4:45 PM, Pacific Time, Monday to Friday.

Priority Support: 900-370-5583
(Automated Hint Line) This is 75¢ per minute and is available 24 hours, 7 days a week.

Hint Fax: 206-562-4223

Fax Support: 206-644-7697

24-hour Automated Technical Support: 206-644-4343

Automated support is available 24 hours, 7 days a week.

Online Computer Support

Computer Support via Sierra's BBS: 206-644-0112 (23 hours a day)

CompuServe:

Sierra ID: 76004,2143

 GO GAMEAPUB

Dynamix ID: 72662,1174

 GO GAMECPUB

Customer Service ID: 70007,1265

Sierra BBS via CS: GO SIERRA

OnLine Mall: GO SI

America OnLine: Keyword: SIERRA

Jim Ferrell of Sierra On-Line

▶ Kings Quest (versions 1–7), Space Quest (versions 1–6), Leisure Suit Larry (versions 1–3, 5, 6), Gabriel Knight, Police Quest (versions 1–4), Lode Runner, Front Page Sports: Football Pro '95, Front Page Sports: Baseball, Phantasmagoria, MetalTech EarthSeige, Alphabet Blocks

"I love the customer contact aspect of this job," says Jim Ferrell. "I always said I'd never work in a cube, day in and day out, same ol' thing, no outside contact. Now that I am in that cube, this job allows me the versatility to meet and talk to folks every day, either on the phone, through E-mail or direct contact. I've developed some lasting friendships with some of our customers online, and that's made it all worthwhile."

Jim Ferrell is the online support administrator and user group coordinator for Sierra On-Line. He is respon-

S

Worldwide Support
United Kingdom: 44-734-303171
   Fax Support: 44-734-303362
   Standard support is available 9 AM to 5 PM,
   Monday to Friday.

   24-hour Automated Technical Support:
   Continental Europe (France): 33-1-46-01-4650
   Hint Fax: 33-1-46-31-7172
   Hint Line: 33-1-36-68-4650
   Hint Lines: 44-734-304004 (older games)
               44-891-660660 (new games)
               44-190-336516 (German line)

   BBS in United Kingdom: 44-734-304227

Sigma Designs, Inc.

▶ Video boards and monitors
▶ Real Magic MPEG decompression board
▶ Winwave, Winstorm, and Winsound Multimedia
   Kits

sible for all online services that Sierra On-Line is pres-
ently on. This includes CompuServe, America OnLine,
the Sierra BBS, and the Internet. Ferrell administers all
dealings with these services including OnLine Malls
through Sierra's direct sales department, organizing
their own forums for private download areas to benefit
the MIS department, and even an overseas contact
point for Sierra's Public Relations department. Ferrell
also oversees all of the customer correspondence with
technical support and customer service via E-mail on
these services.

As the user group coordinator, Ferrell is responsible
for donations to PC user groups to help them raise
money for their clubs and to promote his company's
games. Most user groups have a very large member base
that purchase computer games. Ferrell travels and visits
these users groups, does product demonstrations, teaches
basic principles of computer gaming, and discusses

Continued . . .

Voice, Standard Support: 510-770-0100

Fax Support: 510-770-2905

Online Computer Support

Computer Support via Sigma Designs' BBS: 510-770-0111

CompuServe:
Type: GO DTPVEN (Desktop Publishers Publishing Forum)

Prodigy:

Sigma Designs Imaging Systems

Monitors, video cards, and CPU backplane boards

Voice, Standard Support: 510-770-2900

Fax Support: 510-770-2920

hardware needs and various other computer gaming related topics.

"The part I like least about this job is the chronic complainers," says Ferrell. "It seems that most folks, when writing E-mail, forget their manners and attack me and the company for whatever reason, usually a problem with a product, and expect me to have the exact answer to their problem with the next post." Ferrell says it's virtually impossible to test a product on all IBM computers because of the exponentially varying configurations. Newer sound cards, video cards, and faster CD-ROMs might cause older games to fail: "Sometimes customers don't understand this and can be quite cruel in requesting help for these problems."

Before coming to Sierra, Ferrell played football for the University of Southern Mississippi and spent a short time with the Dallas Cowboys in 1987. He finished his B.S. in computer science with a minor in business from

Online Computer Support

Computer Support via Sigma Designs' BBS: 510-770-8972

CompuServe:
Type: GO DTPVEN (Desktop Publishers Publishing Forum)

Special Information

Sigma Designs Imaging Systems is a Subsidiary of Sigma Designs Inc. and we both share the same building but with a different address. SDIS operates their own sales and support as does Sigma Designs, Inc.

Sir-tech

Voice, Standard Support: 315-393-6644

Standard support is available 9 AM to 5 PM, Eastern Time, Monday to Friday. Support is free. Updates and disk exchanges carry a fee after 30 days.

Athens State College in Alabama in 1992. "I have quite a working knowledge of computers, having built my personal computer from scratch, changing motherboards, adding peripherals, starting in 1986 with an XT to the present with a 486DX 50."

In college, Ferrell worked in the computer lab and helped users with their problems, configured and maintained over 50 computers in the lab and taught lab classes. After graduation, Ferrell worked for a small computer company that sold manufacturing software. "I realized that the company was going nowhere and heard that Sierra On-Line was moving to Seattle. I submitted my resume and was hired two months later! I've been with the company for over a year and have never regretted it. It's a wonderful company to work for."

Ferrell says the most difficult questions that he encounters are from users who assume that he has a list of error codes for every single game sitting on his desk.

Continued . . .

Fax Support: 315-393-1525

Online Computer Support

CompuServe: 76711,33
Type: GO GAMBPUB

Internet: 76711.33@CompuServe.com

Hint Line: 315-393-6633
Hints are available 4 PM to 8 PM, Eastern Time,
Monday to Friday, and on weekends and
holidays, 12 PM to 4 PM.

SoftCraft, Inc.

► SoftCraft Presenter
► SoftCraft Graphic Custom Control for Visual
  BASIC
► Font Solution Pack
► Laser Fonts
► SoftCraft Font Editor
► Fancy Font

"This is not true," he says. "Error codes are put there to
allow a technician or programmer to see a common
problem." However, Ferrell explains that even the most
common problems can take a long time to detect.

"The most common problem that I am asked is
about memory management in DOS and Windows,"
says Ferrell. "So many users do not understand the im-
portance of optimum memory management. I am con-
stantly helping people create boot disks because they
don't have their memory configured correctly on their
machine." Ferrell says that, most of the time, it is not
the customer's fault, but the fault of the computer store
that sold them the machine. "Optimum memory on
any DOS machine, in my opinion, should be around
600K free. This is almost impossible to do with the number of memory-resident programs that are out on the
market today. Mouse drivers, virus detectors, Smart-
Drive, and CD-ROM drivers can all take away from the
precious 640K that is needed to get a game running."

Voice, Standard Support: 608-257-3300

Fax Support: 608-257-6733

Online Computer Support

   E-mail: 76702.1304@CompuServe.com

SoftKey International

- ▶ Calendar Creator
- ▶ WordStar for Windows PhotoFinish
- ▶ PFS: Window Works
- ▶ The American Heritage Dictionary

Voice, Standard Support: 404-428-0008
   Standard support is available 9 AM to 8 PM,
   Eastern Time, Monday to Friday.

Voice Response Unit: 404-514-6330
   Automated 24 hours, 7 days a week

Office Fax: 404-427-1150
   Automated: 404-514-6330

Ferrell says that, as long as there is a computer market, computer game companies will push the PC envelope, demanding better graphics, better sound, higher speed processors, and more memory to make the games more interesting. "Without that edge, we would never sell a game," he says.

As for the customers that Ferrell enjoys the most, he names the ones that take the time to learn the basics about their computers. "We don't expect you to be a computer expert," he says. "Just be able to maneuver in DOS, know what DOS version you have, know what kind of computer you have. Just the basics." Ferrell offers the following tips to help users and their technicians arrive at quick solutions:

1. Give your name and where you are from.
2. Give the name of the game and your system information and briefly discuss the problem that

Continued . . .

Fax-On-Demand (a fax-back service 24 hours, 7 days a week): 404-514-6333

Online Computer Support

Computer Support via SoftKey's BBS: 404-514-6332

CompuServe: Type: GO SOFTKEY

Special Information

SoftKey International is the result of a merger between WordStar International, Spinnaker Software, and SoftKey Software Products. Support is supplied for software produced under those names, as well as software carrying the ZSoft or PowerUp brand.

SoftLogic Solutions, Inc.

- ► @Liberty–1-2-3 compiler
- ► Blackjack Master
- ► Carousel–premier task switcher utility
- ► ClassiFILE–file-handling program

you are having. Include any and all things that you've done to remedy the problem yourself.

3. Listen to the technician and do what he or she asks you to do, even if you already have done it. Sometimes it helps the technician to collect his or her thoughts to come up with the optimum solution for you.

4. Don't be afraid to ask questions. That's what we are here for. If you don't know what is going on, ask and let the technician know that you are uncomfortable with the solution or that you don't understand.

5. "Being a technician is a thankless job some-times," says Ferrell. "Rarely do we get any grati-tude for fixing the problems that we fix. Take a moment to say thanks for the help, and occa-sionally write a letter expressing your gratitude. I really enjoy knowing I made someone happy."

- ▶ Cubit–file-compression software
- ▶ Disk Optimizer for Windows–hard disk unfragment utility
- ▶ Disk Optimizer Tools–unfragments files on a hard disk
- ▶ DoubleDOS–true multitasking software under DOS
- ▶ Fatcat–disk-management utility
- ▶ Help Yourself–Windows help file authoring tool
- ▶ Magic Mirror–data-integration program for data capture and transfer
- ▶ Miser 386–memory-management utility
- ▶ Open Link Extender–network extension to Software Carousel
- ▶ Software Carousel–DOS application switcher
- ▶ WinSense–online information resource of Windows options

Voice, Standard Support: 603-627-9900 or 800-272-9900

Fax Support: 603-627-9610

Online Computer Support

Computer Support via SoftLogic's BBS: 603-644-5556

Sound Deals, Inc.

- ▶ All brands of Midi software or hardware
- ▶ Repair most products brands

Voice, Standard Support: 205-823-4888

Fax Support: 205-979-1811

Spalding

- ▶ DataImport(tm)–file-translation utility
- ▶ ProRep–productivity measurement and reporting system

Spalding

▶ OpRep–operations measurement and reporting system

Voice, Standard Support: 404-449-1634

Fax Support: 404-449-0052

Online Computer Support

   CompuServe: 74431,240
   Type: GO SPALDING (PCSVENE), Section 2 for messages
   Lib 2 for updates and other files

Spectrum HoloByte

▶ Games for PCs, Macs, Super NES, SEGA, 3DO, and Game Boy
▶ FALCON 3.0
▶ Tornado
▶ Tetris series

Voice, Standard Support: 510-522-1164
   Standard support is available 8 AM to 5 PM, Pacific Time, Monday to Friday.

Automated Technical Assistance and Fax-Back System: 800-TECH-958

Fax Support: 510-522-9357

Automated Game Hints line for USA: 900-773-HINT

Automated Game Hints line for Canada: 900-451-3546

Online Computer Support

   Computer Support via Spectrum HoloByte's BBS: 510-522-8909

   America OnLine: Keyword: SHOLOBYTE

   CompuServe: 76004,2144

   GEnie: HOLOBYTE

Prodigy: TKN33A

Internet: 76004.2144@CompuServe.com

Special Information

We do not, at this time, maintain our own Internet FTP site. However, we do attempt to leave all of our latest updates on both of the following anonymous FTP sites: onion.rain.com and ftp.funet.fi.

Specular International

Online Computer Support

America Online: SpecTech2

When sending questions to SpecTech2, please include the following:

Name
Address (U.S. mail)
Phone
AOL address
Serial number (required)

In addition, when presenting problems to Specular via E-mail, it is best to put the problem into perspective. Keep these things in mind:

1. A description of the problem or desired effect.

2. If possible, a scene file with all of the related PICT maps that cause the problem and, where applicable, a PICT demonstrating the problem.

By following these guidelines, Specular can ensure that your questions can be answered in a timely manner.

Spinnaker Software Corp.

- ► ACE–air combat emulator
- ► Alphabet Zoo
- ► Backgammon
- ► Better Working One Person Office–accounting package
- ► Better Working Spreadsheet
- ► Better Working Word Publisher
- ► Calendar Creations: Best Friends, Exotic Cars, Legends of Baseball, Oceans Alive–calendar makers
- ► Certificate Maker
- ► Easy Working Address Book and Label Maker
- ► Easy Working Address Book Maker for Windows
- ► Easy Working Business Letters (DOS)
- ► Easy Working Business Letters for Windows
- ► Easy Working Cards, Signs, and Certificates
- ► Easy Working Desktop Publisher (DOS)
- ► Easy Working Desktop Publisher for Windows
- ► Easy Working Eight-in-One for Windows–integrated software
- ► Easy Working Labels! for Windows–label printing software
- ► Easy Working Mail Manager for Windows
- ► Easy Working Presentation Maker
- ► Easy Working Resume Kit
- ► Easy Working Word Processor
- ► Easy Working Word Processor for Windows
- ► Easy Working: Resume Creator, The Connector, The Filer, The Planner, The Writer, Tri Pack, Typing Teacher
- ► Eight-in-One
- ► Facemaker
- ► Facemaker: Golden Edition
- ► First Publisher Font Library

S

- ▶ Homework Helper Math Word Problems
- ▶ Homework Helper Writing
- ▶ In Search of the Most Amazing Thing
- ▶ Kids on Keys
- ▶ Kidwriter
- ▶ Kidwriter: Golden Edition
- ▶ Kindercomp
- ▶ Learn the Alphabet
- ▶ Learn to Add
- ▶ MasterCook II–recipe collection on disk
- ▶ Personal Access–hypermedia application for Windows
- ▶ PFS: Business Plan, Business Plan for Windows, First Choice, First Graphics, First Publisher, First Publisher Art Gallery (book), First Publisher Business Template Kit, First Publisher Clip Art Portfolio, First Publisher Font Portfolios, Office In a Box, PowerAlbum, Preface, Professional File, Professional Plan, Professional Write, Prospect, Publisher, Resume & Job Search Pro, WindowWorks, Write
- ▶ Pinstripe Presenter
- ▶ Plus–hypermedia authoring tool for Windows
- ▶ Plus Software Lot Developer's Kit
- ▶ Quadralien
- ▶ Resume Kit
- ▶ Riders of Rohan–based on J.R.R. Tolkien's Lord of Rings
- ▶ Sargon 4–computer chess
- ▶ SAT Complete–score-improvement system for the SAT
- ▶ Scoop, The
- ▶ Sky Runner
- ▶ Snooper Troops #1: Granite Point Ghost
- ▶ Snooper Troops #2: Disappearing Dolphin
- ▶ Splash!–paint program

Spinnaker Software Corp.

- ▶ SplashCard
- ▶ Star Tribes: Myth of the DragonLord
- ▶ Stargoose

Voice, Standard Support: 617-494-9148

Fax Support: 617-494-1219

SSI

- ▶ Al Qadim: Genie's Curse–(AD&D) Arabian Game
- ▶ Alien Logic–science fiction role playing
- ▶ Cyclones–first-person shooting game
- ▶ Dark Legions–AD&D meets chess
- ▶ Dark Sun: Wake of Ravenger–AD&D sequel to hit game
- ▶ Menzobarrazan–first-person AD&D
- ▶ Panzer General–WWII wargame
- ▶ Renegade-space combat flight simulator
- ▶ Tanks (Wargame Construction II)–make your own wargame (modern)

Voice, Standard Support: 408-737-6850 or 408-737-6800

Hint Line: 900-737-HINT

Online Computer Support

Computer Support via SSI's BBS: 408-739-6137 (9600 bps)
408-739-6623 (2400 bps)

CompuServe:

America OnLine: StratSim

GEnie:

STF Technologies, Inc.

- ▶ FaxSTF 3.0–fax software for Macs
- ▶ Network version and Optical Character

Recognition (OCR) software
► STF AutoPak for FaxSTF 3.0
► STF PowerFax Personal Edition
► STF's OCR product for FAX documents

Voice, Standard Support: 816-463-2021

Fax Support: 816-463-7958

Online Computer Support

    Computer Support via STF's BBS: 816-463-1131

    AppleLink: D1870

    CompuServe: 74740,1244
    Type: GO STFTECH

    America Online: STFtech or keyword "STF"

Strategic Studies Group

Voice, Standard Support: 904-469-8880
    Standard support is available 9 AM to 5 PM,
    Eastern Time, Monday to Friday.

Fax Support: 904-469-8885

Online Computer Support

    CompuServe: 72662,3471

    GEnie: SSG

    AppleLink: AUST0161

Steinberg/Jones

Voice, Standard Support: 818-993-4161

Fax Support via Fax on Demand: 800-888-7510

Online Computer Support

    Internet: cubasers-users@mcc.ac.uk

SunDisk Corp.

▶ PCMCIA interface
▶ IDE interface
▶ Compact flash

Voice, Standard Support: 408-562-3400
  Standard support is available 8 AM to 5 PM,
  Pacific Time, Monday to Friday.

Fax Support via FaxBack System: 503-967-0072

Online Computer Support

  Computer Support via SunDisk's BBS: 408-986-1186

  CompuServe: Type: GO SUNDISK

Superbase, Inc.

▶ d.b.Express/Superbase
  Edition–report/chart/graph generator
▶ Perspective for Windows–charting and graphics
  program
▶ Superbase–relational database for Windows

Voice, Standard Support: 516-244-1570

Fax Support: 516-244-0250

Supra

Voice, Standard Support:
  503-967-2490 (PCs)
  503-967-2492 (Mac)
  503-967-2440 (other)
  Standard support is available 8 AM to 5 PM,
  Pacific Time, Monday to Friday.

Fax Support: 503-967-2401
  FAXnetwork: 206-905-1555

Online Computer Support

  Computer Support via Supra's BBS: 503-967-2444

CompuServe: Type: GO SUPRA

American OnLine: Keyword: SupraCorp2
faxnetwork

AppleLink: D2456

GEnie: SupraTech

Internet: supratech@supra.com
or faxnetwork@supra.com

Swan Technologies

▶ 486 Vesa local bus
▶ Bicycle series–Poker, Solitaire, Cribbage, and
  Bridge (Win/DOS)
▶ EISA computers
▶ Gettysburg CD–CD-ROM simulation of the battle
  of Gettysburg
▶ Limited Edition–contains both versions of all four
  games
▶ Multimedia PCs
▶ Network file servers
▶ Network workstations
▶ PCSI computers
▶ Typecase volumes I, II, and III–TrueType fonts
  (Wind/Mac)

Voice, Standard Support: 800-468-7926
  Standard support is available 9 AM to 6 PM,
  Eastern Time, Monday to Friday, and Saturdays
  9 AM to 5 PM. Swan's technical support answers
  technical calls concerning hardware, software,
  and just about anything else computer users can
  ask. However, this service is open only to Swan
  computer owners. Swan's technical support line
  is toll free, and their users have technical
  support for as long as they own their Swan
  computer.

Fax Support: 814-237-4450

Online Computer Support

 Computer Support via Swan's BBS: 814-237-6145

 CompuServe: Type: GO SWAN

Special Information

 Swan also offers telephone technical support at
 our toll number 302-234-1750 and fax support
 at 302-234-1760.

Symantec Corp.

Voice, Standard Support: 800-441-7234 (United
 States and Canada)
 503-334-6054 for all other locations
 Standard support is available 7 AM to 4 PM,
 Pacific Time, Monday to Friday. Assistance is free
 for the first 90 days, starting with your first
 phone call. Support thereafter is pay-for-service.

Specific Product Support:

 Norton Desktop, Norton AntiVirus, Norton
 Backup, Symantec AntiVirus for Mac, Fastback,
 other products not listed: 503-465-8420

 Norton pcANYWHERE: 503-456-8430
 Norton Utilities, Public Utilities, Suitcase,
 DiskDoubler: 503-465-8440
 Symantec C++, THINK products: 503-465-8484
 Q&A, Q&A Write, Time Line, all other Symantec
 products not listed: 503-465-8600
 ACT! products: 503-465-8645

Fax Support: 503-334-7400

 Fax On Demand (United States and Canada
 only):
 Symantec's Fax On Demand provides instant
 access to general product information, technical

notes, and virus definitions through a 24-hour automated attendant. To access this service, simply have your fax number ready and dial 800-554-4403 from any fax machine or touch-tone phone.

Priority Support

If you occasionally need to call Technical Support but want priority service when you do call, you'll appreciate Symantec's "pay as you go" PriorityCare Services, which are available in two forms:

PriorityCare 900 Number Service
First minute free, $2 each additional minute (charged to your telephone bill). 900 Service for Network products is billed at $300 per call.

Norton Desktop, Norton AntiVirus, Norton Backup, Symantec AntiVirus for Mac, Fastback, other products not listed: 900-646-0007
Norton pcANYWHERE: 900-646-0006
Norton Utilities, Public Utilities, Suitcase, DiskDoubler: 900-646-0005
Symantec C++, THINK products: 900-646-0003
Norton Administrator for Networks, DiskLock: 900-646-0002
ACT! products: 900-646-0001

PriorityCare 800 Number Service
Charge to your credit card at $25 per call ($300 for Network products). We accept VISA, MasterCard, and American Express.

Norton Desktop, Norton AntiVirus, Norton Backup, Symantec AntiVirus for Mac, Fastback, other products not listed: 800-927-3991
Norton pcANYWHERE: 800-927-4012
Norton Utilities, Public Utilities, Suitcase,

Symantec Corp.

DiskDoubler: 800-927-4019
Symantec C++, THINK products: 800-927-4014
Norton Administrator for Networks, DiskLock:
800-927-4017
Q&A, Q&A Write, Time Line, all other Symantec
products not listed: 800-927-4018
ACT! products: 800-927-3989
All other Symantec products not listed: 800-745-
6055

PremiumCare Service

If you need technical support more than
occasionally, Symantec's PremiumCare plan
might be your best (and more cost-effective)
choice. Offered at two levels (Gold and
Platinum), PremiumCare is available by annual
subscriptions, with each subscription covering
an entire family of Symantec products.

PremiumCare Gold
An unlimited number of toll-free technical
support calls, priority access and quarterly
updates of Symatec's technical notes and
bulletins.

PremiumCare Platinum
Symantec's top service level is designed for
corporate help desk personnel or subject-matter
experts who support Symantec desktop products.
PremiumCare Platinum service lets you
designate two or more subscriber contacts who
will be given priority access to our senior support
staff, additional technical support
documentation and updated quarterlies that
include software revisions, technical notes, and
bulletins.
For subscription prices or to order PremiumCare

Gold or Platinum Service, contact Customer Service at 800-441-7234.

Online Computer Support

Computer Support via Symantec's BBS: 503-484-6669 Technical information is available 24 hours a day on the Symantec BBS. The Symantec BBS provides a Customer Service forum, public-domain software, and product support forums for Symantec software. Settings for the Symantec BBS are 8 data bits, 1 stop bit, and no parity.

To contact the Symantec BBS using 300-, 1200-, and 2400-baud modems, call 503-484-6699 (24 hours).

To contact the Symantec BBS using 9600-baud modems, call 503-484-6669 (24 hours).

CompuServe: Type: GO SYMANTEC at any ! prompt.

America Online: Keyword: SYMANTEC

Worldwide Support

Australia
  Phone: 61-2-879-6577
  Fax: 61-2-879-6594
  BBS: 61-2-879-6322

Brazil
  Phone: 55-11-289-9420
  Fax: 55-11-287-9824

Canada:
  Montreal
  Phone: 514-393-1776
  Fax: 514-393-3314

  Ottawa
  Phone: 613-782-2465
  Fax: 613-782-2364

Symantec Corp.

Toronto
Toll free: 800-667-8661
Phone: 416-366-0423
Fax: 416-366-4453

Vancouver
Phone: 604-737-0214
Fax: 604-737-0219

France
Phone: 33-1-42-04-24-46
Fax: 33-1-46-97-11-32
Serveur ASCII Symantec (US)
Accessible 24h/24 par minitel: 36.16 code
SYMANTEC

Germany
Customer Service
Phone: 49-211-9917-162

Technical Support
Phone: 49-211-9917-110
Fax: 49-211-9917-222

Italy
Phone: 39-22-600-0120

The Netherlands
European Headquarters
Phone: 31-71-353-111
Fax: 31-71-353-150
BBS (1200-, 2400-, and 9600-baud modems): 31-71-353-169
Fax On Demand: 31-71-353-255 (24 hours)

Switzerland
Phone and fax: 41-72-22-80-20
Symantec Upgrade Center
Phone: 41-56-27-92-05
Fax: 41-56-27-92-08
Mailbox: 41-56-27-26-83

Symantec Corp.

United Kingdom
   Phone: 44-628-592-222
   Fax: 44-628-592-393
   Fax On Demand: 44-628-777-435 (24 hours)

United States of America
   Phone: 408-252-3570
   Fax: 408-253-4992
   BBS (300-, 1200-, and 2400-baud modems): 503-484-6699 (24 hours)
   BBS (9600-baud modems): 503-484-6669 (24 hours)

Symptom

Voice, Standard Support: 408-894-1427
   Standard support is available 6 AM to 6 PM, Pacific Time, Monday to Friday.

Online Computer Support

Computer Support via Symptom's BBS:

CompuServe: PCSVENF section 2

Internet
If you send a message to support@xstor.com, provide Symantec with how you want them to contact you, and describe the problem and any configuration information, an incident will be logged into their call-tracking system with a high priority. If you send a message to techconnect@xstor.com, by using some command words, you can access Symantec's knowledge base that they use when customers call them on the phone. For instance if you send a message with the following in the message area:

SYMPTOM XT8760S SYMPTOM HANG SYMPTOM NETWARE

you then will get a message back listing documents that have those symptom words associated with them. You then can send a message requesting specific documents by including "DOCUMENT 11.1234" in the message area of your E-mail to get document 11.1234 or any other document that you specify.

This service really has helped Symantec to improve our response times as well as being available 24/7 365 days a year.

Sytron Corp.

- ▶ ProServe CX
- ▶ ProServe CX Lite
- ▶ Sytos Plus for DOS
- ▶ Sytos Plus for Windows
- ▶ Sytos Plus for OS/2
- ▶ Sytos Rebound
- ▶ Sytos Repro
- ▶ Sytos Scheduler

Voice, Standard Support: 508-898-0193
Standard support is available 8 AM to 7 PM, Eastern Time, Monday to Friday.

Fax Support: 508-898-2677
Fax on Demand: 508-898-0001
SyFax Automated Fax Information Response System: 508-898-0001

Online Computer Support
Computer Support via Sytron's BBS: 508-898-2608

Worldwide Support
Sytron Europe/United Kingdom
Calling from Europe: 44-734-810072
Calling from the UK: 0734-810072
FAX: 44-734-810074

Calling from the United States: 011-44-734-810072
BBS: 44-734-817536

The European business hours are 8 AM to 6 PM, UK Time, Monday to Friday.

The Technology Group, Inc.

▶ General Counsel
▶ XyWrite for Windows
▶ XyWrite 4 for DOS

Voice, Standard Support: 410-576-2040
    Standard support is available 9 AM to 7 PM,
    Eastern Time, Monday to Friday.

Fax Support: 410-576-1968

Online Computer Support

    Computer Support via The Technology Group's BBS:
    410-576-8806

    CompuServe: 74603,761
    There ia a XyWrite discussion group in the IBM
    Applications area in the Word processing forum.

    Internet: Via CompuServe
    Type: lstrv@ccat.sas.upenn.edu (group
    discussion: xywrite@ccat.sas.upenn.edu)

Technology Works

▶ Mac and PC memory products
▶ Windows/CAD accelerator boards
▶ Performance-enhancement products
▶ Windows/Cad Accelerators
▶ Hardware/Software (distributed by: Ingram
   Micro, Merisel, Tech Data, Mac Connection, Mac
   Warehouse, Mac Zone; memory also is sold
   through CompUSA and Babbages)

Online Computer Support

    America Online: TechWorks

Worldwide Support
London: 44-81-747-8666

TeknoSys, Inc.

Voice, Standard Support: 813-620-3494
  Standard support is available 8:30 AM to 5:30
  PM, Eastern Time, Monday to Friday.

Fax Support: 813-620-4039

Online Computer Support

America OnLine: Keyword: TEKNOSYS
The TeknoSys Customer Support Area is
available to all America Online subscribers. The
purpose of the TeknoSys Customer Support Area
is to provide online access with America Online
users. This area contains information to support
customers, developers, dealers, and distributors
with TeknoSys products. It can be used as a
direct connection with TeknoSys, Inc.

If you have questions about the TeknoSys
Customer Support Area, you can send a private
message to TEKNOSYS, attention Troy.

AppleLink: TEKNOSYS

CompuServe: 71333,710

Internet: teknosys@applelink.apple.com

☎ All technical support questions submitted
electronically are processed in the order that
they are received. If it is possible for TeknoSys to
answer your question immediately, you will
receive an answer within 24 hours of the receipt
of your message. If your question cannot be
answered immediately or TeknoSys needs more
information from you, you will receive an
acknowledgment that your mail has been
received and a request for more information
within 24 hours. Responses to questions received
on a Friday will be posted the following Monday.

Worldwide Support

Outside the United States: Dial the international dialing code, the country code for the U.S., then dial 813-620-3494.

Special Information

TeknoSys, Inc. reserves the right to use messages posted on this Customer Support Area in other TeknoSys publications. By leaving a message on the TeknoSys Customer Support Area, you expressly consent to such use.

If you have a problem or technical questions about any TeknoSys product, please post these directly to this board. Answers to these questions will be posted by the TeknoSys Technical Support Staff and other board users, and your question will become visible to others. This also is a chance to stimulate discussion and exchange tips with other users of TeknoSys products.

Telebit

▶ Modems, routers, and communication servers

Voice, Standard Support: 408-734-5200 or 800-TELEBIT (835-3248)
Standard support is available 6 AM to 6 PM, Pacific Time, Monday to Friday.

Fax Support: 408-745-3848
FaxBack System: 408-745-3310

Online Computer Support

Computer Support via Telebit's BBS: 408-745-3861 (PEP)
408-745-3707 (non-PEP)

CompuServe: 75300,2170
In the MODEMV forum (48-hour response)

Internet
FTP: ftp.telebit.com (143.191.3.1)
gopher: (143.191.3.1)
WWW: www.telebit.com
E-mail: support@telebit.com (networking products)
modems@telebitcom (modem products)

NetBlazer: netblazer-users@telebit.com

Applelink: Telebit

America OnLine: Keyword: Telebit TS

Temporal Acuity Products, Inc.

- ▶ MusicPrinter Plus v4.1 for DOS
- ▶ Rhythmaticity v2.0 for DOS
- ▶ PianoWorks v2.2 for DOS
- ▶ Music Lab Series for DOS
- ▶ Guido for DOS
- ▶ Inner Hearing for MAC/Win
- ▶ Nightingale for MAC
- ▶ MicroMusic Software Library for Apple II

Voice, Standard Support: 800-426-2673
Standard support is available 9 AM to 5 PM, Pacific Time, Monday to Friday. TAP provides free support to registered users.

Fax Support: 206-462-1057

Online Computer Support

Computer Support via Washington MIDI Users Group BBS: 703-532-7860
You can obtain information on a local MIDILINK BBS, with this BBS

CompuServe: 71333,1275 (Temporal Acuity Products)
Section 15 of the MIDIBVEN forum

Temporal Acuity Products, Inc.

MIDILINK BBS network
Temporal Acuity Products forum in the
Computer Software/Hardware section of the
Industry Hotline.

Texas Instruments

Standard Support: 800-848-3927
Standard support is available 8 AM to 6 PM,
Central Time, Monday through Friday.

Fax Support: 817-774-6660

TTD Support: 817-774-6582

Three-Sixty

▶ Harpoon II
▶ Victory At Sea
▶ High Command
▶ Harpoon
▶ The Harpoon battle sets 1-4
▶ The Harpoon Designer Series 1 and 2
▶ Megafortress and the two mission disks
▶ Theatre of War
▶ Patriot
▶ Blue Max
▶ Sands of Fire
▶ Warlock
▶ Dark Castle
▶ Insight

Voice, Standard Support: 409-776-2187
Standard support is available 9 AM to 6 PM,
Central Time, Monday to Friday.

Support Hotline: 409-776-2187

Fax Support: 409-776-4216

Online Computer Support

America OnLine: E-mail address: THREESIXTY
On America Online, Three-Sixty supports
message forums for all of our products, and we
have a software library for our game related
software, upgrades, and uploaded information.

Timeslips Corp.

- ▶ Timeslips (Windows, DOS, and Mac)
- ▶ TAL, Timeslips Accounting Link
- ▶ Timeslips Speller
- ▶ Timeslips Remote
- ▶ TimeView (DOS)
- ▶ TimeSheet Professional (Windows and DOS)

Voice, Standard Support: 508-768-7490

All registered users who have sent in their
warranty registration card receive 30 days of free
technical support. The support is free; you pay
only for the phone call. The 30 days begin with
your first phone call or fax to our support
department, not when you register your software
or from the purchase date.

After this initial period, you can continue
receiving technical support only by registering
for one of the following support options.

Option 1: On-Demand Support Plan
Technical support is available on a per-call basis
at a fixed hourly rate. You can choose On-
Demand Support now and change over to a Full
Support plan at a later date, as your support
needs change.

On-Demand support costs:
Single User products: $60/hour with a $10
minimum charge.

Timeslips Corp.

Network Edition products: $100/hour with a $25 minimum charge

Please be prepared to give your credit card (MasterCard or Visa) information to the technical services representative when your call is answered.

Option 2: Full Support Plan
This is a one- or two-year support plan that includes these additional benefits not available to On-Demand customers:
Toll-free technical support phone number
Priority response over all other customers
Extended hours (9 AM to 8 PM ET)
Discount price upon support plan renewal
Special mailings with discounts on products and services
Priority access to the TIMESLIPS Corporation Bulletin Board Service (BBS)

With three distinct product groups, Timeslips, TimeView and TimeSheet Professional, there are three types of full support plans available to best serve your needs. Contact Timeslips for pricing information.

Regular Full Support–covers one of the three product groups
Gold Full Support–covers any two of the three product groups
Platinum Full Support–covers all three product groups

For installations with more than 50 licenses, contact TIMESLIPS Corporation's Sales Department at 800-285-0999, ext. 6.

Fax Support: 508-768-7532
If you are on a support plan or are within your

free support period, you can fax your questions to the Technical Support fax machine 24 hours a day. These faxes generally are answered immediately but will always be answered within one business day. Please include your serial number and as much information about your problem as possible. Timeslips' response is always by fax.

Online Computer Support

Computer Support via Timeslips' BBS: 508-768-7581 The BBS contains tips and recommendations from technical support representatives, updated printer drivers, product demos, third-party links, useful utilities and much more. Questions, comments, and suggestions can be left on the BBS and will be answered each day.

Online Computer Support

CompuServe:

America OnLine:
For online Timeslip support, contact Richard Levesque at screen name TS RICHARD.

Timeworks

► 4 in 1 Art Portfolio (PC, Apple II)
► Data Manager (PC, Commodore)
► Design Ideas (PC, Apple II)
► Education Graphics (PC, Apple II)
► Evelyn Wood Dynamic Reader (PC, Commodore)
► Font Packs (Apple II)
► People, Places & Things (PC, Apple II)
► Publish It Lite! (PC)
► Publish It! (PC, Apple II)
► Publish It! Easy (Macintosh)
► Swiftcalc (PC, Commodore)

Timeworks

- ▶ Symbols & Slogans (PC, Apple II)
- ▶ Word Writer (PC, Commodore)
- ▶ Word Writer Pro (PC)

Online Computer Support

America Online: Timeworks5

Trend Micro Devices, Inc.

- ▶ Antivirus and Security Products for PCs and LANs

Voice, Standard Support: 310-782-8190

Online Computer Support

Computer Support via Trend's BBS: 310-320-2523

CompuServe: 72662,432
Type: GO PCSVENE
Select TREND MICRO DEVICES,INC

Trio Information Systems

- ▶ Datafax
  All Trio's products include a "support and customer feedback" program called comment. This can be used to generate direct "faxes" to a special 800 number that transfers user information/system and set-up/questions in a special high-speed manner.

Voice, Standard Support: 919-846-4985

Fax Support: 919-846-4997

Online Computer Support

Computer Support via Trio's BBS: 919-846-4987
(North America)
46-8-570-35-290 (Europe)

E-mail: support@trio.com

CompuServe: Type: GO TRIO

TRIUS, Inc.

Voice, Standard Support: 508-794-0140
Standard support is available 9 AM to 4 PM,
Eastern Time, Monday to Friday. When you
register or upgrade TRIUS software, you
automatically are entitled to three months of
free technical support and newsletters. Registered
users can extend this period of basic technical
support and newsletters for $25 per year. To help
Trius solve your problem quickly, please be at
your computer, know the program and DOS
versions, as well as your PCS system
configuration when you call.

Fax Support: 508-688-6312

Online Computer Support

Computer Support via Trius BBS: 508-794-0762
This service is provided free of charge to
registered users. You pay only your telephone
charges. Technical support, a user forum, and
current versions of all our shareware programs
are available for download.

Technical Bulletins now are posted on the BBS.
These are collections of Questions and Answers
from newsletters and frequently asked Technical
Support Questions. These bulletins are available
for download in the TRIUS Programs directory.

CompuServe: 71333,103
Type: GO TRIUS at any CIS prompt.
PCS VENDOR F Forum, Section 16

Special Information
In addition to TRIUS' programs, the BBS also
contains files that have been uploaded by Trius
users. These range from simple to complex

worksheet templates and macros, complex
DRAFT Choice and ProtoCAD 3D drawings, and
utility programs. These files generally are self-
extracting compressed files or files that were
compressed using PKZIP. You will need to have
PKUNZIP to decompress the ZIP files. While
TRIUS doesn't evaluate the files, it is definitely
worth a visit to the "Other Programs" directory
to see what's there. You also are encouraged to
upload files.

Tseng Labs, Inc.

▶ ET1000 monochrome adapter controller
▶ ET2000 Super EGA chip set used on the EVA,
  EVA/480, and NEC GB-1 adapters
▶ ET3000 Super VGA chip
▶ ET4000 Super VGA chip

Online Computer Support

E-mail: TsengJoeC, TsengRonMc
Any customer using any Tseng Labs video
controllers is permitted access to this area and
the use of all files there. Access to the Tseng Labs
private area is restricted to Tseng OEMs only. To
gain admittance to the Tseng private area, please
send an E-mail to TsengJoeC, TsengRonMc, or
call Tseng Labs at 215-968-0502.

TurboPower Software

Voice, Standard Support: 719-260-6641 (Pascal
  products)
  719-260-1681 (C++ products)
  Technical support is free to registered customers.

Fax Support: 719-260-7151

Online Computer Support

Computer Support via TurboPower's BBS:
719-260-9726

CompuServe: 76004,2611 (Pascal products)
75300,2214 (C++ products)
PCSVENB section 6 (Pascal products)
PCSVENE section 1 (C++ products)

Internet FTP:
rainbow.rmii.com:/pub2/turbopower

Special Information

Maintenance patches and public domain
extensions for TurboPower products can be
downloaded from the CompuServe forums, by
Internet FTP, and from the TurboPower BBS.

Twelve Tones Systems, Inc.

▶ Cakewalk 5.0–DOS-Based sequencing software
▶ Cakewalk Professional 3.0–Windows 3.1
  sequencing software
▶ Cakewalk Home Studio–Windows 3.1 sequencing
  software for PCs
▶ Cakewalk Apprentice for Windows–Entry-level
  sequencer

Voice, Standard Support: 617-924-6275

Fax Support: 617-924-6657

Underware

▶ Track Record

Voice, Standard Support: 617-267-9743
Support is available 9 AM to 5 PM, Eastern Time, Monday to Friday.

Fax Support: 617-424-1839

Online Computer Support

CompuServe: Type: GO UNDERWARE

Internet: track_record@uw.com

US Robotics

▶ Sportster 28.8 V.34 w/fax
▶ Sportster 28.8 V.34 PC w/fax
▶ Sportster 28.8 V.24 MAC & fax
▶ Sportster 14.4 PCMCIA w/fax
▶ Sportster 28.8 PCMCIA w/fax
▶ Courier V.34 Ready Data/Fax w/V.FC
▶ Courier V.34 Data/Fax w/V.FC
▶ Courier Dual Standard 28.8 PCMCIA w/fax

Voice, Standard Support: 708-982-5151
Standard support is available 8 AM to 6 PM, Central Time, Monday through Friday

Fax Support: 708-933-5552

Fax on Demand: 800-762-6163
The USR fax-on-demand system is a 24-hour automated fax system that can supply information about technical and nontechnical issues. Call into the system to have a menu of documents faxed to you, then select the specific document that you need from the menu.

Online Computer Support

Computer Support via US Robotics' BBS:
708-982-5092

CompuServe: Type: GO USROBOTICS

Internet: Type: support@usr.com

Worldwide Support
International
Phone: 011-33-2019-1959
Fax: 011-33-2005-3240

Vedit

Voice, Standard Support: 313-996-1300
   Vedit offers free technical support to any
   registered user of their products for one year.
   Vedit asks only for their serial number to confirm
   registration.

Online Computer Support

   Computer Support via Vedit's BBS: 313-996-1304

   CompuServe: Type: GO VEDIT
   PCS VENDOR I forum, section/library 5.

Velocity, Inc.

► Spectre VR CD-ROM (PC)
► Remind Me (Mac)
► Network Remind Me
► Jet Ski Rage

Voice, Standard Support: 415-392-4357
   Voice support is available 9 AM to 4:30 PM,
   Pacific Time, Monday to Friday. Technical
   support is provided for all registered users.

Fax Support: 415-928-3299

Online Computer Support

   Computer Support via Velocity's BBS: 415-274-8853
   This is Velocity's customer online 24-hour
   modem-to-modem service. Customers will be
   able to download demo disks to their computer
   and obtain public relations materials, the latest
   ads, promos sales sheets and company catalog,
   etc.

Vertisoft Systems

► Emulaser
► Amidiag

V

- ▶ Superprint
- ▶ Turbotype
- ▶ Font Encyclopedia

Voice, Standard Support: 800-466-5875
Specific products have individual support phone
numbers:
Emulaser: 803-269-6446
Amidiag: 404-246-8645
Superprint: 714-851-2191
Turbotype: 803-269-9969
Font Encyclopedia: 803-269-9969

Fax Support: 800-466-4719

Special Information
Vertisoft cannot provide voice callbacks from
messages posted online, so please don't ask.
Also, Vertisoft prefers to receive all questions in
the AOL support area, rather than by E-mail.
However, there are questions and sensitive
information that are best sent and responded to
via E-mail (addresses, phone numbers,
invoice/customer numbers). Please use the E-
mail address "Vertisoft" for E-mail messages.

Vertisoft tries to limit the number of folders in
the message area to specific topics. If you do not
find the appropriate folder, please use the
Miscellaneous Messages. Vertisoft will either
create a new folder or transfer your message to
the appropriate one. They also will inform you
of such via E-mail so that you know what
happened to your message. Also, many times a
question is posted for which there already is a
response on the message board. Please review
the appropriate folders relative to your software
or support issue. If you do not find your answer

Vertisoft Systems

in these, then post a message. Vertisoft spends a lot of time removing duplicate messages, so your help and consideration in this matter is appreciated. If you don't get a response quickly enough (i.e., you post on Monday and still haven't been answered by Wednesday), don't hesitate to post reminders.

Viacom New Media

- ▶ On Cue II
- ▶ Sherlock Holmes, Consulting Detective–CD-ROM-based interactive video game series
- ▶ Dracula Unleashed

Voice, Standard Support: 303-339-7114
Standard support is available 8 AM to 7 PM, Central Time, Monday to Friday.

Fax Support: 303-339-7022

Online Computer Support

CompuServe: 76702,1604
Type: GO CDROM

America OnLine: VNM Support

AppleLink: VNM

Videodiscovery

- ▶ Interactive multimedia for K-12 science and math
- ▶ Videodisc programs–high-quality visuals
- ▶ MediaMAX

Voice, Standard Support: 800-548-3472 or 206-285-5400

Fax Support: 206-285-9245

Online Computer Support

America OnLine: Keyword: Videodiscovery
You can download MediaMAX slideshows and lessons that other teachers have made. Read about our comprehensive image databases (such as Bio Sci II and Anatomy & Physiology), our interactive programs (such as Science Sleuths, Math Sleuths, and STS Forums), and new products coming soon. You also can contact Videodiscovery through our message board, and they will respond to your questions on education and technology within 24 hours.

Viewpoint DataLabs

▶ Dataset–3D data representation of physical objects

Voice, Standard Support: 801-224-2222

Fax Support: 801-225-2999

Virgil Corp.

▶ StockTracker

Voice, Standard Support: 415-433-9025

Fax Support: 415-433-8411

Online Computer Support

CompuServe: 71333,3667

Internet: 71333.3667@CompuServe.com

Virtual Reality Laboratories

▶ Vistapro
▶ Makepath
▶ Vistamorph
▶ Distant Suns

▶ Mars Explorer

Voice, Standard Support: 805-545-8515 or 800-829-VRLI

Fax Support: 805-781-2259

VNM

Online Computer Support

    America OnLine: VNMSupport

    Internet: vnmsupport@icomsim.com

Voyager Company

▶ Multimedia CD-ROMs for Mac and PC
▶ Expanded books for Mac
▶ Videodiscs, videotapes, and videodisc companion software
▶ CD companion programs
▶ Audiotapes

Voice, Standard Support: 914-591-5500

Fax Support: 212-431-5799

Online Computer Support

    America Online: Keyword: VOYAGER

Voyetra Technologies

Voice, Standard Support: 914-966-0600

Fax Support: 914-966-1102

Online Computer Support

    Computer Support via Voyetra's BBS: 914-966-1216
    The BBS has multiple lines.

GEnie and others:

Internet: 76702.2037@CompuServe.com
voyetra@aol.com
voyetra_tech@delphi.com and
voyetra@delphi.com

Voyetra Technologies

Wacom Technology Corp.

► ARTZ-SERIAL–6" × 8" digitizing tablet
► PL100V–integrated (pen/display) tablet (DOS and Windows)
► SC100–four-button cursor (puck) for all other SD Series
► SC510–four-button cursor (puck) for SD-510C tablet only
► SD-210L–18" × 25" digitizing tablet
► SD-310E–12" × 18" digitizing tablet
► SD-311E–12" × 18" electrostatic surface
► SD-312E–12" × 18" menu panel dig
► SP200–ASD series nonpressure stylus
► SP300–SD series firm pressure stylus
► SP310–SD series soft pressure stylus
► UC420–four-button cursor (puck) for all UD Series tablets
► UD-1212RP–12" × 12" menu panel tablet
► UP201–UD series pressure stylus

Voice, Standard Support: 206-750-8882

Fax Support: 206-750-8924

Online Computer Support

   Computer Support via Wacom's BBS: 408-982-2737

   America Online:
   In the Wacom Forum, you can receive support and information on Wacom Technology products, as well as download current Wacom tablet drivers and product information.

Warpspeed Computers

► The Graham Utilities for OS/2

Voice, Standard Support: 61-3-384-1060

Fax Support: 61-3-386-9979

Online Computer Support

Computer Support via Warpspeed's BBS:
61-3-386-3104

CompuServe: OS2AVEN Other Vendors section

FidoNet: 3:632/344 (Brunswick VIC 3056)

Internet: 100250.1645@CompuServe.Com

Worldwide Support

Australia
Phone: 02-904-1988
Fax: 02-953-9401
CompuServe: 100250,1645

Germany
Phone: 089-1405322
Fax: 089-1405623

Westech Corp.

Voice, Standard Support: 800-745-4378 (U.S. and
Canada)
201-729-4378 (International)
Standard support is available 9 AM to 6 PM,
Eastern Time, Monday to Friday. Westech
generally answers a support question on the first
call, and their average call length is 6 minutes.
They charge a minimum of three minutes for a
chargeable call and do not charge support time
for problems that are caused by software bugs in
their program.

Fax Support: 201-729-0431

Online Computer Support

Computer Support via Westech's BBS: 201-729-9468

CompuServe: 72662,1641
PCVENJ, Section 5

Internet: E-mail address:
72662.1641@compuserve.com

Special Information

A customer receives 60 days of toll-free (from United States and Canada) and unlimited technical support from the date of contact for a "key code," which Westech's security system that prevents multiple sites from using their software, while not limiting the number of copies a licensed user can run.

After 60 days, users purchase telephone support time in blocks of one hour or one half hour. For users in the United States, one hour of toll-free technical support costs $90, and one half hour is $52.50.

In Canada, because of increased expense on Westech's 800 calls from there, Westech charges a surcharge of 45¢ per minute (incoming or outgoing calls) to cover this additional expense, making charges $66 for 30 minutes and $117 for 60 minutes. Because Westech cannot offer toll-free support to other countries, they apply a discount reflecting their 800 number costs (about 15¢ per minute) making incoming technical support cost $48 for 30 minutes or $87 for 60 minutes. When Westech has to call or fax the other countries, they charge a factor determined by their telephone rate to that country on top of the per minute charge.

Westwood Studios

- ▶ Command & Conquer
- ▶ DUNE: The Battle For Arrakis (Sega Genesis)
- ▶ DUNE II
- ▶ Kyrandia 3: Malocolms Revenge
- ▶ Lands of Lore: The Throne of Chaos
- ▶ Lands of Lore II
- ▶ The Legend of Kyrandia
- ▶ The Lion King for the Sega, Genesis and Super Nintendo
- ▶ Young Merlin (Super Nintendo)

Voice, Standard Support: 714-833-1999
Standard support is available 8 AM to 5 PM, Pacific Time, Monday to Friday.

Hint Line: 900-288-4744
Canada: 900-451-4422

Automated Fax Support: 714-833-1999

Online Computer Support

Computer Support via Westwood's BBS: 702-368-2319

Internet: 71333.2405@CompuServe.com

CompuServe: 71333,2405
Go to GAMBPUB and select the Westwood Studios Conference

America OnLine: Keyword: PC GAMES
Select Company Support and select Westwood Studios

GEnie: WESTWOOD

Prodigy: NTBU56B
Jump to "Software Connexion" and select Westwood Studios

Willies Computer Software Company

Voice, Standard Support: 713-983-9427

Fax Support: 713-568-3334

Online Computer Support

Computer Support via Willies' BBS: 713-568-6401

Internet: support@wcscnet.com

CompuServe: 75300,3427
Type: GO EWILLIES (PCSVENF Section 5)

Fidonet E-Mail: 1:106/14

Wilson WindowWare, Inc.

▶ WinEdit Lite
▶ File Commander
▶ WinBatch

Voice, Standard Support: 206-937-9335
The first hour of support is free.

Fax Support: 206-935-7129

Online Computer Support

Computer Support via Wilson's BBS: 206-935-5198

CompuServe: 76702,1072
In forum WINAPA, data library 15
Type: GO WILSON

America OnLine: Keyword: WINDOWWARE
WWWTECH@aol.com

Internet: ftp.www.windowware.com
/wwwftp/wilson
76702.1072@CompuServe.com

World Wide Web:
http://www.windowware.com/wilson/pages

WindSoft International, Inc.

▶ Accounting software
▶ Restaurant management software (POS System with hardware integration)
▶ Bottom Line Accounting, version 3.1

Voice, Standard Support: 407-240-2300

All new purchases receive 90 days of free support. After 90 days, free support still is available by fax, mail, and CompuServe.

Fax Support: 407-240-2323

Priority Support:

The 90-day plan is $99 and includes free unlimited support by phone, fax, mail, and CompuServe.

The 1-year plan is $199 and includes free unlimited support for 12 months and same benefits as the 90-day plan.

The pay-as-you-need plan is $2 per minute with a minimum of $10 per call.

Online Computer Support

Compuserve: 75300,562
Type: GO WINDSOFT at any ! prompt

Working Design

▶ CD:LUNAR
▶ The Silver Star
▶ VAY
▶ Popful Mail
▶ LUNAR:Eternal Blue

Voice, Standard Support: 916–243-3417
> Phone support is limited to advice and tips. For maps, hint books are available for prices ranging from $13.95 to $19.95.

Fax Support: 916–243-3157

World Software Corp.

▶ Document management software for DOS and Windows
▶ WORLDOX for Windows
▶ Extend-A-File Plus for DOS

Voice, Standard Support: 201-444-3290
> Standard support is available 9 AM to 5 PM, Eastern Time, Monday to Friday. World Software provides free support to licensed users.

Fax Support: 201-444-9065

Online Computer Support
> *CompuServe:* PCS Vendor I Forum

Xceed Technology

- ▶ Add-in products
- ▶ 8-bit and 24-bit graphics cards for the Mac
- ▶ HP LaserJet printer memory
- ▶ Other memory products for both Macs and PCs

Voice, Standard Support: 800-642-7661 or
   800-XCEED-IT

Fax Support: 810-598-8008

Online Computer Support

   America Online: Keyword: XCEEDTECH

Xircom, Inc.

- ▶ Network adapters

Voice, Standard Support: 800-874-4428
   Standard support is available 5 AM to 6 PM,
   Pacific Time, Monday to Friday. Twenty-four hour
   automated services provide access to installation
   instructions, technical bulletins, a user forum,
   and the latest software drivers.

Automated Services: 805-376-9020
   24 hours a day, 7 days a week

Fax Support: 805-376-9100
   FactsLine Information Retrieval: 800-775-0400
   The Technical Support fax machines can be called
   24 hours a day, 7 days a week. Xircom generally
   responds to incoming faxes for technical support
   by the end of the following business day. Please
   indicate your name, your company's name, your
   fax number, and your voice telephone number on
   your fax. Also, please give as much of the
   following information as you can:

   Product model number
   Product description

Xircom, Inc.

Network operating system (NOS)
Topology (Ethernet, token-ring, etc.)
Driver filename
Hardware (your computer make, model, speed, style)
Software
Symptoms
Question or problem

Online Computer Support

Computer Support via Xircom's BBS: 805-376-9130
To access Xircom's bulletin board, you will need a modem and communications software set up to 14,400 bps, no parity, 8 bit, and 1 stop bit (N-8-1). Xircom's BBS modems will adjust automatically to lower speeds. Set your terminal emulation to TTY or ANSI (VT terminals are not supported).

Using a modem, you can access technical and product information and download the latest versions of Xircom's network drivers. You also can leave a message for Technical Support and receive a response within two business days.

CompuServe: Type: GO XIRCOM
Using a modem, you can access the same type of information found on Xircom's FactsLine and BBS, plus you can access their CompuServe Forum and scan messages from other users and Xircom's technical support staff. Messages left for Technical Support will receive a response within one business day.

Internet: cs@xircom.com

Worldwide Support
Canada (Ontario)
Voice, Standard Support: 800-565-3284

Standard support is available 8:30 AM to 5 PM, Canadian Eastern Time, Monday to Friday.

Fax Support: 905-479-0232
Online and Automated Services:
24 hours a day, 7 days a week. Dial your local international access code +1+805-376-9020.
BBS: Dial your local international access code +1+805-376-9130.

Europe, Middle East, and Africa
Voice, Standard Support: +32/(0)3.360.38.60
Standard support is available 8:30 AM to 5:30 PM, Monday to Thursday, and to 4:30 PM on Friday.

Fax Support: +32/(0)3.326.31.50
Online and Automated Services:
+32/(0)3.360.38.00
24 hours a day, 7 days a week
BBS: +32/(0)3.326.23.68

Asia/Pacific (Hong Kong)
Voice, Standard Support: 852-2525-2078
Standard support is available 9 AM to 5 PM, Monday to Friday.

Fax Support: 852-2525-8955

Online and Automated Services:
24 hours a day, 7 days a week. Dial your local international access code +1+805-376-9020.
BBS: 852-2537-6048

Young Chang America

Voice, Standard Support: 310-926-3200
Standard support is available 8 AM to 5 PM,
Pacific Time, Monday to Friday. Operational
support also is available at 516-689-7728,
between 9 AM to 6 PM, Eastern Time, Monday to
Friday.

Fax Support: 310-404-0748

Online Computer Support

CompuServe: Kurzweil Section in the MIDI Vendor
A forum.

PAN: There is a Kurzweil SIG.

MIDILINK: There is a Kurzweil Section.

America OnLine: Kurzweil section in the Music
and Sound area

Internet: Kurzweil@aol.com or E-mail at the
CompuServe address

Special Information
Technical support for Kurzweil products is
provided for all Kurzweil instruments except for
the K250. All support and service for that
product are done by Sweetwater Sound at 219-
432-8176.

Z

ZCI

Voice, Standard Support: 214-746-5630

Standard support is available 9 AM to 5 PM, Central Time, Monday to Friday. Support is free to all registered ZCI customers.

Fax Support: 214-746-5560

Online Computer Support

CompuServe: 71333,2741
Type: GO ZCIPUB

Zenith Data Systems

- ▶ Z-NOTESLEX laptop computer
- ▶ Z-STAR-EX laptop computer
- ▶ Z-STATION 510 desktop
- ▶ Z-SELECT PT desktop

Voice, Standard Support: 800-227-3360

Standard support is available 24 hours, Monday to Friday.

Fax Support: 708-808-4468

Fax in a basic description of your problem with your product's model number and serial number. Include your phone number, and Zenith will call you back.

Online Computer Support

Computer Support via Zenith's BBS: 708-808-4942

Worldwide Support

Singapore: 65-22-44133
Poland: 48-22-48-55-04
Israel: 972-3-751-55-11
The standard 800-808-4468 number will direct all international assistance needed.

Zeos International

▶ Pantera Ambra Systems
▶ Pentium 90 Computer
▶ Notebooks 800c, 400c
▶ Meridian Notebooks
▶ Software (sent with machine):
Lotus 1, 2, 3
Word for Windows Group
MS DOS 6.22

Voice, Standard Support: 800-228-5390
Standard support is available 24 hours, 7 days a week, including holidays. For international support, call 612-362-1222. Canada is 800-228-5390.

TT/TTD Support: 800-228-5389

Fax Support: 612-633-4607
Factfax also is available at 800-845-2341. You can fax for software revision changes or hardware problems.

Online Computer Support

Computer support via Zeos BBS: 612-362-1219

CompuServe: Keyword: GO ZEOS

Internet: Type: SUPPORT@zeos

Zoom Telephonics, Inc.

▶ Modems

Voice, Standard Support: 617-423-1076

Fax Support: 617-423-9231
Standard support is available 8:30 AM to 11 PM, Eastern Time, Monday to Friday, and 9 AM to 5 PM, Saturday.

Online Computer Support

Computer Support via Zoom's BBS: 617-423-3733

CompuServe: 76711,770

ZyPCsom, Inc.

▶ Modems and multiplexers
▶ Z34 (28.8K modem)
▶ Z32 T-SX (19.2K modem)
▶ Z32 B-SX (14.4K modem)

Voice, Standard Support: 510-783-2501
Standard support is available 8 AM to 5 PM,
Pacific Time, Monday to Friday.

Fax Support: 510-783-2414

Appendix

Troubleshooting Guide

This appendix includes steps that you can take to try to troubleshoot your computer problems before you call technical support. There are two main sections: one for DOS and the other for Windows.

Troubleshooting techniques for DOS

Whenever you have a problem with a DOS program, it can be broken down and identified usually in one of the following ways.

Check for sound card problems

Usually when you are using a program or application that uses sound, you will want to check the system for sound problems. Sound cards use interrupt request lines (IRQs) to communicate with the central processor. If you have two devices that are trying to use the same interrupt, a lock-up can occur. A common problem is having the sound card set for IRQ 7 and the printer set for LPT 1. Most folks don't realize that IRQ 7 is the same as LPT1, thus causing a lock-up when both devices are in use. The best way to check for a hardware conflict is with DOS's MSD (Microsoft Diagnostic) program, which is included with DOS versions 6.0 and greater.

Check for any hardware conflicts on the system. An easy way to do this is to rerun the install program from the software directory on the hard drive and choose No Audio/Voice Card for the Audio option. If the program works with no audio, there might be a sound card setting conflict. Many sound cards come with utilities that can check for hardware conflicts.

Please consult your sound card documentation for more information on test utilities.

Use CHKDSK

The best diagnostic tool available in DOS is the CHKDSK or SCANDISK command. Occasionally, a hard drive will get corrupted. Lost allocation units, crosslinked files, and file allocation table errors can be common if you don't check the disk and fix these before they get ugly. DOS provides a utility that will do this for you. In the earlier versions of DOS, that command is CHKDSK. When this command is executed, it checks the integrity of the hard drive and reports if there are problems found. Once the problems are found, you first should back up any irreplaceable data from the affected hard drive. To correct lost allocation units or other errors on the hard drive, use the CHKDSK /F command, or any other disk diagnostics utility such as PC Tools, Norton Utilities, or SCANDISK. Consult your MS-DOS or Disk Utility manual for more information. Once you have corrected these hard drive errors, delete any files associated with the program from your hard drive, verify that you have plenty of free hard drive space and re-install the program from the original disks.

One problem with using CHKDSK /F is that, once the problems are fixed, you might have problems with the files that were corrupted, and applications that ran before might not run now. To illustrate this, imagine you have a loaf of bread, let that loaf of bread represent a file. Let's say that ⅓ of the loaf gets mold on it. Then you, noticing the mold, take a knife and remove the mold so that the rest of the loaf is okay. Well now you have a loaf (file) that is not complete, and depending on what was on the part that was cut away, this file might or might not work properly when accessed again by the system. The solution here is to delete the file and copy it back as it was originally, basically baking a new loaf identical to the old one.

Another popular utility is SCANDISK, which is included in DOS version 6.2+. SCANDISK is the same as CHKDSK but is a bit more thorough. It allows you to make corrections without having to run the program again. It also will allow you to do a surface test. A surface test basically checks for physical errors on the hard drive itself. If physical errors are found, the undamaged files/bytes are moved to an undamaged area, the area will be marked as bad in the file allocation table, and the computer will no longer use that portion of the hard drive. Unfortunately, any files residing on the bad sector of the hard drive will be lost forever. Again, you will want to delete the files and copy them back over to be sure that all the files are there.

Check hard disk space

Hard drive space can be another area to check when troubleshooting a problem. Today, most programs that are shipped on floppies come with compressed files. What are compressed files? Compressed files are files that have been shrunk with a compression program to approximately half their original size. This takes up less disk space, allowing companies to ship a product on 5 floppies instead of 10. The problem arises when an end user has an "on-the-fly" compression program running on his/her system. These are programs that will compress the hard drive and seemingly double the amount of hard drive space available. In most cases, this can be a good idea; however, in today's market, with companies shipping products that already are compressed, it can be quite confusing.

Let's say you have a 20MB file that has been compressed to 10MB and put on 4 disks. If not compressed, would have fit on 8 disks. There are 2 hard drives that this file can be installed to: a 20MB hard drive and a 10MB hard drive that has been doubled with a compression program so that it now also has 20MB. When the file is installed to the 20MB hard drive, it installs just fine. However, when the file is loaded on the 10MB drive, it fits, but with no space left after the file is loaded to the hard drive. The reason is that a compressed file, in a compressed environment, takes up space equal to its original size: 20MB. When running with less than 100MB of compressed space, it's best to be sure that you have double the hard drive requirements for the product; otherwise it's possible that not all of the program was installed properly, which could be causing the problem.

Making a boot disk

Making a boot disk is the single most important step when troubleshooting. The premise of the boot disk is to get back to the basics. It's a known fact that the program giving you problems was tested and ran under a standard system configuration. Your system configuration, CONFIG.SYS and AUTOEXEC.BAT files on the C: drive, were set up to run your machine. It is not a good idea to try and make system changes to these files in an attempt to get a program to run. You could possibly lock your system up pretty good, and not be allowed access back to it. If you don't know what you are doing, *never* change your system configuration.

Fortunately, IBM-compatible systems give us a way to get around this. When booting the computer, you will note that the system checks the A: drive first, then the C: for the system configuration. Basically it's looking for commands on what to load to get the computer running. By creating a boot floppy, you can make the system bypass your usual startup files and use the ones provided on the A: drive instead. This allows you to make changes without the fear of locking up the system. Should a lock-up occur, simply remove the boot disk, and the system will use the system, or C:, configuration, which has not changed.

When using a boot disk, you can load only the files that are needed for the program to run. Other TSRs or memory-resident programs—such as SMART-DRV, DOSKEY, ANSI.SYS, etc.—will not have to be loaded and a basic configuration can be made. The following are instructions on making a boot disk.

Step 1: Formatting the disk
Note: It is necessary to format the disk even if the disk already has been formatted. The /S switch will transfer files to the boot disk that are necessary for the disk to work correctly. To make a boot disk, format a high-density diskette in the A: drive. (Use the /F:360 or /F:720 parameter if you are using a low-density diskette.) For more information on using the FORMAT command, consult your DOS manual. *Note*: This will not work in the B: drive. Type the command as follows:

```
FORMAT A: /S
```

If, after entering this command the system responds with a "Bad command or file name" error, then type:

```
PATH=C:\DOS
```

Now retype the previous FORMAT command. If you still receive the same error, the MS-DOS FORMAT command might not be on your system or it might have been renamed. Programs such as PC Tools and

Norton Disk Utilities can rename the FORMAT command to prevent accidental data loss. If you are using a program like this, check your documentation to find out how to format a system disk, then go to Step 2.

Step 2: Locating the mouse drivers
If you are going to use a mouse in your program, you will need to load the mouse driver with the boot disk. To do this, locate the mouse driver and copy it to the boot disk in your A: drive. There are two types of mouse drivers available, MOUSE.SYS, which must be loaded in the CONFIG.SYS file, and MOUSE.COM (MOUSE.EXE on some systems), which must be loaded in the AUTOEXEC.BAT file. You do not need to load both MOUSE.SYS and MOUSE.COM. Locate the MOUSE.SYS or MOUSE.COM file. Because the file MOUSE.SYS usually is smaller than MOUSE.COM, we recommend that the MOUSE.SYS file be used to free more memory.

Locating the mouse drivers. If you do not know where the MOUSE.SYS or MOUSE.COM files are located on your system, the following command should help in locating your mouse drivers. Type the following at the C:\> prompt:

```
DIR \MOUSE* /S
```

On systems using DOS or later, this command will cause the system to search all of the subdirectories for a file called MOUSE. If the system locates a file called MOUSE, it will display the path where the mouse files are located. For instance, if the MOUSE.SYS file is located in the C:\MOUSE directory, the system will display:

```
Directory of C:\MOUSE
        MOUSE SYS       55160  03-10-92 3:10a
        MOUSE COM       56408  03-10-93 6:00a
```

Troubleshooting Guide

If the system does not locate a mouse, your driver might have a different name or these files might not be currently installed on the system. Some other common names for mouse drivers are IMOUSE, GMOUSE, and HPMOUSE. Your mouse drivers might have been included on a floppy disk that came packaged along with your mouse. For information on the proper name for your driver, check the owners manual that came with your mouse.

Copying the mouse driver. Once you have located the mouse driver, you will need to copy it to the boot disk. In this step, we will assume that the mouse drivers were located in the C:\MOUSE directory as shown in the previous step. To copy the MOUSE.SYS file to the boot disk, type the following at the C:\> prompt:

```
COPY C:\MOUSE\MOUSE.* A:
```

Please substitute the appropriate path and filename for your mouse driver in the previous command. You then should see a message indicating that some files were copied.

Step 3: Locating the MSCDEX CD-ROM extension
MSCDEX is the Microsoft extension for CD-ROM drives. It must be loaded for your CD-ROM drive to operate. The following steps should assist you in locating this file on your system. To locate MSCDEX, at the C:\> prompt, type:

```
TYPE AUTOEXEC.BAT | MORE
```

Note: The | is called a "pipe" filter and is created by pressing Shift and the backslash (\) key.

Now look for the line that loads MSCDEX. This line should look something like one of these:

```
C:\DOS\MSCDEX /D:MSCD001
LH C:\DOS\MSCDEX /D:MSCD001
```

Appendix

```
LOADHIGH /L:14429 \DOS\MSCDEX /D:MSCD001
```

Your line might differ from these. Write down the entire line following the drive letter. Be sure to include the full drive and path to your MSCDEX file. For example, any of the previous lines should appear as follows:

```
LH C:\DOS\MSCDEX /D:MSCD001
```

Step 4: Locating the CD-ROM device driver
Along with MSCDEX, the CD-ROM also needs a device driver. This driver is loaded in the CONFIG.SYS file. To determine the correct CD-ROM device driver, type the following command at the C:\> prompt:

```
TYPE CONFIG.SYS | MORE
```

Note: If you have a SCSI CD-ROM drive, there might be an additional driver in your CONFIG.SYS that must be run for the CD-ROM device drivers to load correctly. Check your CD-ROM drive documentation for more information.

Now look for the line that contains the CD-ROM device name that immediately follows the same /D: switch as the MSCDEX line in the AUTOEXEC.BAT file. Using the previous example, you would be looking for a line containing MSCD001. This line should look something like one of the following lines:

```
DEVICE=C: \DRV\CDROMDRV.SYS./D:MSCD001
/P:
220
DEVICEHIGH=C:\DRV\CDROMDRV.SYS
/D:MSCD001 /P:220
DEVICEHIGH /L:14652 =C:\DRV\CDROMDRV.SYS
/D:MSCD001 /P:220
```

Your line might differ from these. Write down the entire line following the drive letter. Be sure to include the full drive and path to your CD-ROM device driver.

For example, any of the previous lines should appear as follows:

```
DEVICEHIGH=C:\DRV\CDROMDRV.SYS /D:MSCD001
/P:220
```

Step 5: Creating the CONFIG.SYS file
Now switch to the A: drive and type the following:

```
COPY CON CONFIG.SYS
```

The cursor then will drop down one line. Now type the following lines:

```
DEVICE=C:\DOS\HIMEM.SYS
DEVICE=C:\DOS\EMM386.EXE NOEMS
FILES=30
BUFFERS=20
DOS=HIGH,UMB
LASTDRIVE=Z
```

If you're using a CD program, add the CD-ROM driver line as you wrote it down in Step 4. If you are using the MOUSE.SYS file to load your mouse, add the following line to the CONFIG.SYS:

```
DEVICEHIGH=A:\MOUSE.SYS
```

If you have compressed your hard drive with DoubleSpace or DriveSpace, add the applicable line:

```
DEVICEHIGH=C:\DOS\DBLSPACE.SYS
/MOVE
DEVICEHIGH=C:\DOS\DRVSPACE.SYS
/MOVE
```

Complete the file by pressing Ctrl-Z or the F6 function key and then pressing Enter.

Step 6: Creating the AUTOEXEC.BAT file
Now create an AUTOEXEC.BAT file by typing:

```
COPY CON AUTOEXEC.BAT
```

Appendix

The cursor then will drop down one line. Now type the following lines:

```
ECHO OFF
SET COMSPEC=C:\COMMAND.COM
PROMPT SIERRA CD BOOT DISK $_$P$G
PATH=C:\;C:\DOS;C:\WINDOWS;
```

If you're using a CD program, add the MSCDEX line as you wrote it down in Step 3. If you are using the MOUSE.COM file to load the mouse, add the following line to the AUTOEXEC.BAT file:

```
LH A:\MOUSE.COM
```

Complete the file by pressing Ctrl-Z or the F6 function key and then pressing Enter.

Step 7: Reboot the system
Reboot your system by depressing the reset button on your computer or by using the Ctrl–Alt–Del key sequence on your keyboard. Once you receive an A:\> prompt, go to your hard drive and follow the instructions to begin the program.

Reinstall the program

Sometimes a program can have a problem if it is not installed properly. Whenever a problem occurs and the other troubleshooting steps do not work, it is always best to delete the program completely and reinstall. (It is highly recommended that you re-install after booting up with a boot disk and running CHKDSK /F or SCANDISK.) Be sure to watch for any error messages that might pop up during the installation.

Mouse drivers

Checking to be sure that you have the latest mouse driver for your brand mouse also is a great troubleshooting step.

Incompatible mouse drivers can cause graphics distortion, lock-ups, and other problems. If the program that you are using does not require a mouse, try creating a boot disk and REM out the mouse line in either the CONFIG.SYS or AUTOEXEC.BAT file on the boot disk. Otherwise, try using a different mouse driver or contacting the mouse manufacturer for more troubleshooting information. Sierra recommends using Microsoft mouse driver 8.20 or higher.

CD-ROM drivers

The popularity of CD-ROM titles has added a step to the troubleshooting process. CD-ROM drives *and* discs also should be cleaned periodically to ensure smooth data flow and less problems with the hardware.

Outdated CD-ROM drivers can cause lock-ups, pauses, and CD-ROM read errors, among other errors. Make sure you are using MSCDEX version 2.23 in your AUTOEXEC.BAT. If you're using DOS 6.2 or higher, you will find MSCDEX 2.23 in the DOS directory. If you are not using DOS 6.20, your CD-ROM drive manufacturer should be able to provide you with MSCDEX 2.23. You also should check with your CD-ROM drive manufacturer to make sure that you have the latest version of your CD drivers in your CONFIG.SYS.

Windows troubleshooting

Be sure that no other applications are running before you install or use the program. To check, hold down the Ctrl key and hit the Esc key. This will bring up the Task List. If anything other than the Program Manager shows up on this list, select it and click on

End Task. Repeat these steps until nothing but the Program Manager shows up on the list. Are you using any alternative desktops in Windows? Software such as Navigator, Norton Desktop, Dashboard, and Tab Works can interfere with the program. Try running Windows with the Program Manager. Check your desktop documentation for more information.

Sound-related Windows programs (like Icon Hear It, Wired for Sound, and Packard Bell Navigator) also can cause conflicts with some programs. You should make sure that no program of this type is running at the same time as the program you are installing. You also should check the documentation for your sound card to make sure that the sound card settings are the same in Windows as they are in DOS.

In addition, you should run the MS-DOS CHKDSK to check for lost allocation units or other errors on your hard drive. (If you have MS-DOS 6.2, use the SCAN-DISK program.) If MS-DOS reports that any errors were found, then you should correct the allocation table problems. First, back up any irreplaceable data from the affected hard drive. To correct lost allocation units or other errors on the hard drive, use the CHKDSK /F command or any other disk diagnostics utility such as PC Tools, Norton Utilities, or SCANDISK. Consult your MS-DOS or disk utility manual for more information. Once you have corrected these hard drive errors, delete any files that are associated with that program from your hard drive, verify that you have plenty of free hard drive space, and reinstall the program from the original disks. If you are using any disk compression such as Double Space, you will need twice as much free hard drive space as the program normally uses.

You also should check with your video card and sound card manufacturers to make sure that you have the latest versions of your Windows video and sound drivers. Some manufacturers update their drivers sev-

Troubleshooting Guide

eral times a year, so it's easy to get behind. Outdated or incompatible drivers can cause conflicts with some programs in Windows. If you're using a CD-ROM program, check with the CD-ROM drive manufacturer for driver updates as well.

If the previous steps fail, try creating a Windows boot disk and running the program under the boot disk environment. The following steps will create a Windows boot disk that should work on your system. *Note*: Please read all of the instructions prior to starting at Step 1.

Step 1: Formatting the disk

Note: It is necessary to format the disk even if the disk already has been formatted. The /S switch will transfer files to the boot disk that are necessary for the disk to work correctly.

Format a high density diskette in the A: drive. (Use the /F:360 or /F:720 parameter if using a low-density diskette.) For more information on using the FORMAT command, consult your DOS manual. *Note*: This will not work in the B: drive. Type the command as follows:

```
FORMAT A: /S
```

If, after entering this command, the system responds with a "Bad command or file name" error, then type:

```
PATH=C:\DOS
```

Now retype the previous FORMAT command. If you still receive the same error, the MS-DOS FORMAT command might not be on your system or might have been renamed. Programs such as PC Tools and Norton Disk Utilities can rename the FORMAT command to prevent accidental loss of data.

Step 2: Locating the MSCDEX CD-ROM extension

MSCDEX is the Microsoft extension for CD-ROM drives. It must be loaded for your CD-ROM drive to operate. The following steps should assist you in locating this file on your system. To locate MSCDEX, at the C:\> prompt, type:

```
TYPE AUTOEXEC.BAT | MORE
```

Note: The | is called a "pipe" filter and is created by pressing Shift and the backslash (\) key.

Now look for the line that loads MSCDEX. This line should look something like one of these:

```
C:\DOS\MSCDEX /D:MSCD001
LH C:\DOS\MSCDEX /D:MSCD001
LOADHIGH /L:14429 \DOS\MSCDEX /D:MSCD001
```

Your line might differ from these. Write down the entire line following the drive letter. Be sure to include the full drive and path to your MSCDEX file. For example, any of the previous lines should appear as follows:

```
C:\DOS\MSCDEX /D:MSCD001
```

Step 3: Locating the CD-ROM device driver

Along with MSCDEX, the CD-ROM also needs a device driver. (*Note*: some CD-ROM drives require a SCSI driver. The SCSI driver must be loaded in CONFIG.SYS. Please check your documentation for more information.) This driver is loaded in the CONFIG.SYS file. To determine the correct CD-ROM device driver, at the C:\> prompt type:

```
TYPE CONFIG.SYS | MORE
```

Now look for the line that contains the CD-ROM device name that immediately follows the same /D: switch as the MSCDEX line in the AUTOEXEC.BAT file. Using the previous example, you would be look-

Troubleshooting Guide

ing for a line containing MSCD001. This line should look something like one of the following lines:

```
DEVICE=C:\DRV\CDROMDRV.SYS /D:MSCD001
/P:220
DEVICEHIGH=C:\DRV\CDROMDRV.SYS /D:MSCD001
/P:220
DEVICEHIGH /L:14652 =C:\DRV\CDROMDRV.SYS
/D:MSCD001 /P:220
```

Your line might differ from these. Write down the entire line following the drive letter. Be sure to include the full drive and path to your CD-ROM device driver.

Step 4: Creating the CONFIG.SYS file

Now switch to the A: drive and type the following:

```
COPY CON CONFIG.SYS
```

The cursor then will drop down one line. Now type the following lines:

```
DEVICE=C:\WINDOWS\HIMEM.SYS
STACKS=9,256
BUFFERS=20
FILES=50
BREAK=ON
LASTDRIVE=Z
```

Note: MS DOS 6.0 users who have compressed the hard drive using DoubleSpace or Stacker 3.1 need to add the appropriate line that follows.

For DoubleSpace, add: DEVICE=C:\DOS\DBL SPACE.SYS /MOVE

For Stacker 3.1, add: DEVICE=C:\STACKER\STAC HIGH.SYS

Now add the CD-ROM driver line as you wrote it down in Step 3. Complete the file by pressing the F6 function key and pressing Enter.

Step 5: Creating the AUTOEXEC.BAT file

Now create an AUTOEXEC.BAT file by typing:

```
COPY CON AUTOEXEC.BAT
```

The cursor will drop down one line. Now type the following lines:

```
SET COMSPEC=C:\COMMAND.COM
PROMPT SIERRA CD BOOT DISK $_$P$G
PATH=C:\;C:\DOS;C:\WINDOWS;
```

Now add the MSCDEX line as you wrote it down in Step 2. Complete the file by pressing the F6 Function key and pressing Enter.

Step 6: Reboot the system

Reboot your system by depressing the reset button on your computer or by using the Ctrl–Alt–Del key sequence on your keyboard. Once you receive an A:\> prompt, go to your hard drive and follow the instructions to begin the program. You might want to delete and reinstall the program under the boot disk environment.

If the problems still persist, feel free to call the Technical Support Department of the software program that you have. They are there to help you and will appreciate your efforts to solve the problem yourself. When you contact them be sure to have the following information:

▶ CPU type (286, 386, 486, etc.)
▶ Type of graphics (VGA, EGA, etc.)
▶ DOS version (MS-DOS 6.2, MS-DOS 5.0, PC DOS 4.0, DR DOS 6.0, etc.)
▶ Total RAM memory in your system (1MB, 2MB, 4MB, etc.)
▶ Whether or not you have tried using a boot disk
▶ Largest executable program size or bytes free

Troubleshooting Guide

287

after booting with the boot disk (type MEM or
CHKDSK to find out)
► Whether or not your system has a sound card
(Pro Audio Spectrum, Ad Lib, Sound Blaster, etc.)

Also, please let them know if you are using any
of the following programs:

► DoubleSpace, Stacker, SuperStor, Xtra Drive, or
any other disk compression program
► PC Tools or Norton Mirror program
► Windows (Please state which version)

Also, please restate the situation that you are
experiencing in detail and list the troubleshooting
steps that you have tried. Remember that tech support is there to help you.

Index

Index

Index

Index

Index

Index

Index

About the authors

Bill Adler, Jr. is the president of Adler & Robin Books, Inc., a Washington, DC literary agency. He is the author of over a dozen books, including *Outwitting Squirrels* and *Baby-English: A Dictionary for Interpreting the Secret Language of Infants*, which he wrote with his then 16-month-old daughter, Karen. Adler's first computer was an Atari 800; he then moved up to an IBM PC that came with an extraordinary 128K of memory and two 5¼" floppy drives. He now runs a Pentium-processor based computer, which surely will be replaced by the time this book is published. Adler is on the phone with technical support all of the time. In his spare time, Adler flies aerobatic airplanes, entirely without the assistance of computers.

Kristy Fraser is a native San Franciscan and resides in Washington, DC where she is a freelance journalist and an editor at Adler & Robin Books, Inc. She also is a contributing writer to *Portfolio* magazine and is coauthoring a book on Washington's street crime with an M.P.D. detective. Fraser is an honorary recipient of the *1993 L.A. Times Story of the Year* awarded by the National Collegiate Press Association for her story on the 1992 Los Angeles riots and inner-city youth. Although she had hoped to install sound effects from her stereo computer speaker system into this book for the amusement of her readers, she finds support technicians quite amusing themselves, sort of.